SUCCESS IN SELLING
Developing a World-Class Sales Ecosystem

Reza Sisakhti

PRESS

ATD Press is an internationally renowned source of insightful and practical information on talent development, workplace learning, and professional development.

ATD Press
1640 King Street
Alexandria, VA 22314 USA

Ordering information: Books published by ATD Press can be purchased by visiting ATD's website at www.td.org/books or by calling 800.628.2783 or 703.683.8100.

Library of Congress Control Number: 2015954216

ISBN-10: 1-60728-321-2
ISBN-13: 978-1-60728-321-8
e-ISBN: 978-1-60728-322-5

ATD Press Editorial Staff
Director: Kristine Luecker
Manager: Christian Green
Community of Practice Manager, Sales Enablement: Roxy Torres
Developmental Editor: Kathryn Stafford
Text Design: Maggie Hyde and Iris Sanchez
Cover Design: Tony Julien
Printed by United Graphics, LLC, Mattoon, IL

CONTENTS

CONTENTS

PREFACE

Kayla has been tasked with researching options to solve a particularly sticky problem her company is dealing with. She is sitting at her desk and on her computer she has five windows open and each window has the specs pulled up for different software solutions. She's reading a Twitter feed on her phone because she's crowdsourcing information about how others in her industry have dealt with this problem. She has scoured all of the "about us" boilerplate language on each company's website, and has done some additional research on their corporate responsibility statements (because that's important to her). She's also checked out the LinkedIn pages for each of the companies, in addition to a few other crowd-sourced review sites.

Kayla isn't ready to talk to a salesperson yet, but when she is, she's coming to the conversation fully armed with information. She knows what she thinks she needs and what the competitive landscape looks like.

Welcome to the world of sales in the age of the tech-savvy, socially connected, empowered buyer.

Technology and the rise of the empowered buyer are creating seismic shifts in the world of business—shifts that are impacting how businesses operate and make money. And it is precisely this atmosphere that led us to re-evaluate and update the ATD World-Class Sales Competency Model.

Success in Selling: Developing a World-Class Sales Ecosystem explains the research behind the model and outlines a new competency-based framework for sales talent development. To understand why this update is necessary, it's important to understand how we got here.

When we introduced the first sales competency model in 2008, the reality of the sales professional was very different from what it is today. Twitter was only two years old. If you wanted to log on to Facebook, you had to visit new.facebook.com because the company was introducing The New Facebook, redesigned around "the feed" feature with less prominence on individual profile elements. The company had not yet gone public and was not selling advertising. LinkedIn had just introduced company profiles and launched its first enterprise application, Recruiter, a tool for corporate recruiting teams to source candidates across the entire LinkedIn network. The platform was nowhere near the prospecting machine it is in 2015.

The computers we used were different, too. A late 2007 article in *Computerworld* titled "Personal Tech 2008: Top 10 Trends" noted that the "space between cell phones and laptops remained up for grabs" and said the whole category of tablet-like products was a "wasteland of failed products and confused consumers." Mobile technologies were nascent, and social selling didn't exist as it does today.

The 2008 World-Class Sales Competency Model addressed a landscape for sales professionals unlike what we now see. That reason alone dictated it was time for ATD to update this model. But more has changed than just the landscape in which sales professionals operate.

Today, we have a deeper understanding of what it means to have a sales ecosystem—the interdependent relationships that make sales efforts successful: within sales teams, between sales teams and their colleagues at work, and the relationships buyers have with brands. Being competent in sales isn't only about knowing your product and how to talk to people. Much more is required.

For this update, our team looked at sales functions and the entire ecosystem of sales as it currently exists. This is a highly practical, applicable model. In fact, the ATD World-Class Sales Competency Model is the only publicly available model that covers the entire sales ecosystem.

The research behind the 2015 World-Class Sales Competency Model included a comprehensive review of trends that are shaping the sales profession and how they impact what sales professionals need to know and do to be successful now and in the future. Twelve key trends were noted, and they are grouped into four trend categories: Market Dynamics and Changing Customer Demands, Advances in Technology, Workforce Configuration, and Sales Talent Development. Today, the changing landscape for both sales teams and customers is viewed through a multigenerational, multi-industry global lens.

This 2015 model is more refined and actionable. Twelve areas of expertise are identified and aligned to the three major role categories in the sales ecosystem. You can clearly see what knowledge and skills are required for a specific type of role, whether you are in a leadership, management, or sales strategy role. The model makes it clear that there is a career progression in the sales ecosystem. We believe that one of the strengths of this model is that it works for individuals and organizations. You can apply it to an individual sales person, or you can design your sales ecosystem with this model.

Foundational competencies—those skills that must exist for any sales professional to be successful—are also clearly identified. Clustered in four categories—Collaboration, Insight, Solution, and Effectiveness—these are the building blocks that all sales professionals rely on, and should work to enhance over the course of their careers.

Also included in this update are case studies with real-life connections between theory and application. These studies, combined with global, multi-industry, and multigenerational perspectives, make this book a highly relevant resource for every sales professional, sales function, and organization—regardless of location, industry, or sector. We are extremely proud of all who contributed to this effort.

I hope you enjoy reading *Success in Selling: Developing a World-Class Sales Ecosystem*; I believe you will find this updated competency model and the research behind it informative, relevant, and useful in helping you achieve even greater impact in the work you do.

Wishing you world-class sales results!

Tony Bingham

President and CEO
Association for Talent Development (ATD)
December 2015

ACKNOWLEDGMENTS

The new World-Class Sales Competency Model is the result of contributions from a large number of people. I would like to express my gratitude to:

- **59 thought leaders and sales practitioners** in various industries worldwide, who graciously participated in one-on-one interviews to explore evolving sales practices and their impact on the competencies needed by sales professionals today and in the foreseeable future. Many of these individuals also participated in the validation process by reviewing an earlier version of the new model and sharing their constructive feedback.

- **295 sales professionals** from various regions of the world, industries, and generations, who participated in the validation survey, the results of which were used to revise and finalize the new model.

- **Roxy Torres,** Sales Enablement Community manager at ATD and program manager for this effort, whose resourcefulness, leadership, collaboration, and timely review and feedback made completion of this work possible. Roxy was a pleasure to work with and a great collaborator throughout the process.

- **Jennifer Naughton,** senior director, credentialing, at ATD, who throughout the process shared her timely insights and cumulative wisdom from leading the creation of various competency models for ATD over the years. Her contribution was invaluable.

- **The ATD research team,** especially David Frankel, who were instrumental in implementing a large-scale, complex validation survey with agility.

- **Tony Bingham,** the president and CEO of ATD, who throughout the process provided constructive feedback while constantly challenging us all to build a best-in-class sales competency model.

- Last but not least, my team at Productivity Dynamics—**Alison Fox, Joyce Nadeau, Rande Neukam, Katherine Rathbun,** and **Deborah Smith**—who supported the collection, analysis, and reporting of the research data and who helped construct and validate the competency model. I am grateful for their camaraderie and never-failing willingness to go the extra mile to complete this complex initiative.

INTRODUCTION

Sales has always been a dynamic profession. Today's fluid business environment, however, is characterized by disruptive business practices, ever-changing customer needs and demands, the emergence of new market opportunities, dramatic technological advances, and a continuing reconfiguration of the sales force. Both sales organizations and sales professionals need to monitor the business landscape continuously in order to identify needed business-essential competencies. To help support that effort, ATD has revised and updated the World-Class Sales Competency Model (WCSCM), its original sales competency model.

In 2008, ATD created the first WCSCM and published the book *World-Class Selling: New Sales Competencies* the following year. In addition to establishing a solid understanding of the areas of expertise (AOEs) and foundational competencies needed by all members of the sales ecosystem, the book provided guidelines and tools for building a world-class sales force. The ATD WCSCM has been used by organizations around the world as a powerful tool in a variety of sales talent management efforts, such as attracting, assessing, selecting, engaging, developing, retaining, and credentialing sales and sales enablement professionals and managers.

Beginning in the summer of 2014, ATD undertook another comprehensive research effort using the same methodology to revise and update its 2008 WCSCM, based on evolving trends and sales practices. This new book, *Success in Selling: Developing a World-Class Sales Ecosystem,* presents a description of the research approach, details how the new trends and sales practices are shaping the sales profession, and introduces the new model by describing its architecture and content. It explains the many ways that sales organizations and professionals can implement the model and provides a set of tools, guidelines, and case examples for its effective use.

Intended Audience

Success in Selling: Developing a World-Class Sales Ecosystem is intended for all members of the sales profession from those on the front line of selling to those managing and developing sales talent to those creating other sales enablement solutions. The new ATD model offers sales organizations and professionals a state-of-the-art competency framework and standards to support their talent management goals. In addition to detailed information about the model—the required skills, knowledge, and actions, as well as their relative importance for success—this book also offers sample outputs that show examples of tangible outcomes. In addition, the guidelines, tools, and templates help all readers adapt the new model and use it in the context of any organization. The book is primarily focused on three audiences: sales professionals, sales managers and executives, and sales talent developers and other enablement professionals.

Sales Professionals

The first audience for this book includes individual sales contributors. The new WCSCM enables all members of the sales profession to assess and identify their competency strengths and development needs and to prepare competency development plans to improve their job performances and advance their careers.

Sales Managers and Executives

Sales managers and executives are responsible for recruiting, hiring, onboarding, developing, coaching, motivating, and rewarding sales and sales enablement professionals. The new WCSCM describes the detailed skills, knowledge, actions, and foundational competencies that are required for their success. In addition, it provides guidelines and templates for completing the following tasks, whether individually or in collaboration with a sales enablement team:

- writing or updating job descriptions
- creating hiring guides to screen and select job applicants
- creating assessment tools to define the learning and development needs of their teams
- formulating or revising career paths
- preparing curriculum maps and learning descriptions
- coaching team members on the skills, knowledge, and actions required for success.

Sales Talent Developers and Other Enablement Professionals

These professionals are responsible for defining the skill development needs of the sales organization and for defining, designing, developing, deploying, and evaluating learning and development solutions. They are also responsible for recruiting, hiring, onboarding, and motivating sales professionals. They can use the descriptions of competencies in different AOEs and the descriptions of the foundational competencies needed by all members of the sales ecosystem in the following ways:

- preparing and implementing assessment tools to define the learning and development needs of sales and sales enablement professionals at individual, group, and organizational levels
- coaching team members on the skills, knowledge, and actions required for success
- creating sales learning road maps and learning solutions descriptions to:
  - provide guidelines and requirements to training development and delivery teams to develop new learning solutions
  - assess, select, and revise existing learning solutions
  - evaluate the effectiveness and business impact of learning solutions.
- developing a workforce planning strategy by aligning talent development and selection practices
- creating hiring guides to screen, select, and hire sales talent.

Organization of This Book

Success in Selling: Developing a World-Class Sales Ecosystem is organized into eight chapters and seven appendices. Chapter 1 articulates the value proposition for the new ATD WCSCM, presenting case examples to illustrate key trends that are shaping the sales profession, and introduces the research methodology used to create the new model. Chapter 2 examines in detail the key trends shaping the sales profession, describing the "perfect storm" of forces that are requiring organizations to rethink their sales talent development practices. Chapter 3 introduces the architecture and content of the new model and compares its usability to the 2008 WCSCM. Chapter 4 describes the 12 AOEs unique to each role within the sales ecosystem and how they are aligned to the three major role categories. Chapter 5 details the foundational competencies that are common to all members of the sales profession. Chapter 6 provides guidelines on how organizations can use the new model; guidelines for individuals are detailed in chapter 7. Chapter 8 describes how organizations can customize and adapt the new model to their own needs.

The appendices contain comprehensive details of the model and provide tools and guidelines for its use. Appendix A offers detailed descriptions of the AOEs, including their definitions, key knowledge areas, skills, actions, and sample outputs. Appendix B describes the foundational competencies and their organization into four clusters. Appendix C details the steps used to collect and analyze data to build and validate the new model. Appendix D reports the practitioners' survey results, including participant demographics and a summary of survey responses. Appendix E provides organizations with a tool set (job aids, templates, and guidelines) to build assessments and identify competency gaps and strengths at individual, work group, and organizational levels. Appendix F presents step-by-step instructions and a template for building hiring guides for screening and selecting sales talent for an organization. Lastly, Appendix G provides individual sale professionals with guidelines, templates, and tools for conducting self-assessments and building personal development plans.

1

VALUE PROPOSITION FOR THE NEW ATD WCSCM

Sales professionals are often challenged to articulate the value of a proposed solution, so it is fair to question the value of the new ATD World-Class Sales Competency Model (WCSCM). This chapter explores the following questions and articulates the value proposition for the new model for customer-facing sales people, sales managers and leaders, and sales enablement professionals by examining the qualities of the new model, while listing its limitations and describing in greater detail the research methodology that was used in its creation.

- Why does the sales profession need another competency model?
- What is unique and different about this model?
- Can it help my team and me to identify and close deals with agility?
- Can it help us beat the competition and increase our share of wallet in an account?
- Can it help us enhance the loyalty and commitment of our channel partners?
- Can it help us recruit, select, and hire sales talent?
- Can it help with onboarding, coaching, and developing more productive sales teams?
- How can I be sure that these competencies are the right ones? Do they have a reasonable shelf-life?
- How can I use this model to help my organization achieve its business objectives?

At its core, the new model consists of a set of business-essential competencies needed by all members of the sales profession both today and in the near future to achieve significant business results. The new model, similar to its predecessor (2008 WCSCM), has been developed using a solid research methodology, which is the hallmark of ATD's approach to competency modeling. The new model is user friendly and provides concrete guidelines and tools to support various talent management tasks, such as attracting, selecting, engaging, assessing, retaining, and continuously developing sales talent.

Qualities of the New Model

To enhance its usefulness to organizations and individual sales professionals, the new model features competencies that are business essential and future oriented. The model is based on research from a wide range of organizations from throughout the world that are engaged in many different types of activities, so the model is comprehensive. Its three-part architecture enhances its usability, and it is scalable to organizations of various sizes. It is also adaptable through customization to various industries, geographies, and strategic priorities.

Featuring Business-Essential, Future-Oriented Competencies

The new model contains business-essential competencies needed for success both today and in the near future. The skills, knowledge, and behaviors described in the model are shaped by emerging trends that are influencing the sales profession and are based on in-depth interviews conducted with leading sales practitioners worldwide. These experts were asked to:

- Describe the challenges they face in their everyday practices and the methods they and their teams use to meet these challenges effectively.
- Detail the key competencies that are essential for success not only today but also in the future.
- Provide examples of how these competencies have been used in their organizations and the outcomes. These examples show how application of these competencies has helped to enhance revenue, grow share of wallet, increase the size and velocity of the pipelines, boost commitment and loyalty of channel partners, and improve sales talent development practices and the outcomes of those practices.

Table 1-1 lists case examples aligned to various areas of expertise (AOEs), based on real-world situations where these AOEs and foundational competencies have been applied.

Table 1-1: Case Examples Aligned to AOEs

AOE 1 New Account Acquisition Case 1	**Background:** An account manager is in charge of business development for a consulting firm that provides products and services to clients in the banking industry. **AOE in Action:** In the past two years, the account manager has used LinkedIn to connect with more than 100 senior executives in banks around the world. He posts weekly insights on challenges and opportunities in the banking industry. His postings elicit comments from dozens of executives. With help from a part-time assistant, he follows the executives in his network, providing perceptive comments and practical advice on their postings and questions. He also has an active presence on Twitter, with more than 9,000 followers. **Business Results:** His smart use of social media has been a big contributing factor to his business development success: year-over-year revenue growth in 2014 of 113 percent.

AOE 2 Account Development and Retention Case 2	**Background:** A global account manager (GAM) in the PC and printing division of a Fortune 500 company is in charge of growing and retaining global accounts. **AOE in Action:** With help from her sales operations and IT teams and assistance from the purchasing department of a client, she was able to collect and mine data on the purchase of printers and supplies (paper, ink) by the client worldwide. Armed with insights about the patterns of the client's purchases, she challenged the client's ad hoc and distributed purchasing activities, making a business case for creating a global agreement to consolidate all their spending and provide on-demand online ordering, versus purchasing from local retailers and keeping inventories in multiple locations. **Business Results:** The proposed solution provided the client with an annual cost saving of more than 20 percent, higher quality products, and the convenience of online ordering in all their locations worldwide. The new agreement enabled the GAM to capture almost 100 percent share of wallet of the customer in this area and blocked competitors from the account for at least three years. Her data mining and timely and proactive use of the insights she gained were a catalyst for her success.
AOE 3 Complex Solution Definition and Positioning Case 3	**Background:** A global manufacturing company develops leading-edge solutions that meet and exceed industry standards and the productivity demands of its customers. **AOE in Action:** A new air compression product was recently produced, based on feedback from customers and sales teams, to achieve greater efficiency and lower life-cycle costs for customers. The new solution, however, was offered at a 30 percent higher price point compared with the solution it was replacing. For the company to maintain market share, the sales team needed to become engaged in solution and insight selling to position the new solution with current customers and potential prospects by demonstrating its value to customers' KPIs. During the pursuit phase, presales consultants and sales specialists focused on their buyers' business contexts and challenges. They articulated the impact of the new air compression solution on resolving their productivity challenges. They created prototypes to prove the concept and demonstrate their solution's tangible impact. **Business Results:** By articulating the value of the product in tangible terms, the sales team was able to exceed their initial order forecast and establish a new goal of doubling sales volume (from $10 million to $20 million) for the new solution.
AOE 4 Partner Sales Support Case 4	**Background:** A channel account manager (CAM) in the healthcare and insurance industry manages relationships with a dozen insurance brokers and is responsible for their success in achieving revenue targets. **AOE in Action:** In 2013 the CAM started a structured joint business planning (JBP) effort with his brokers, providing them with clear revenue goals and allocating resources and market development funds (MDFs) to them for achieving those goals. Using a newly implemented CRM system, he started tracking and mining data on their revenue contribution and use of MDFs. He shared insights gained from this analysis with the brokers in monthly review sessions, and they worked together to make the necessary adjustments to the use of funds and to perform other needed activities to achieve the revenue goals. **Business Results:** There was clear improvement in 2014. In one case, a broker achieved 120 percent of her annual quota within the first nine months of the year. The majority of the brokers have demonstrated greater commitment and loyalty to the company. The CAM attributes his success to the use of JBP and the utilization of CRM data to track and analyze MDF investment.

(continued)

Table 1-1: Case Examples Aligned to AOEs (continued)

AOE 5 Sales Pipeline and Forecast Management Case 5	**Background:** A newly promoted sales manager has had a long career as an individual contributor in the field sales organization. **AOE in Action:** Despite his past tendency to take an intuitive approach to forecasting, based on day-to-day experience in the field, the sales manager has rigorously applied new techniques around pipeline management, finding that the new, structured approach is extremely beneficial for building and shaping his team's pipeline as well as for helping accelerate opportunities through the pipeline. In addition, he has pushed his sales team to be disciplined about entering all of their opportunities into the organization's CRM system as soon as possible. **Business Results:** The team's forecast has become more accurate and predictable. In the past, the forecast variance was about 10 percent. After implementing the new forecasting approach, the variance has decreased to less than 3 percent.
AOE 6 Sales Strategy Definition and Execution Cases 6 & 7	**Case 6:** **Background:** A sales manager in a global manufacturing company is based in China. Her local market has many low-end, low-price competitors, making it challenging for her team to compete on a cost-based model. **AOE in Action:** The sales manager was able to leverage her knowledge of the local market, along with her company's global market intelligence resources, to determine which customers may be best suited for the high-end products of the company. For example, in one customer segment, the sales team began to focus their strategy on the added-value services, efficiency, and energy savings that their solutions provide, compared to the cheaper local alternatives. In another customer segment, the sales manager was also able to identify and propose a new, cheaper product offering (less focused on efficiency) to help the team "play and penetrate" the lower-end regional market. **Business Results:** Using real-market insights, the sales manager was able to devise an effective sales strategy and lead her team to exceed their quota by optimizing their presence in the market. **Case 7:** **Background:** An account executive for a global services firm had a goal to expand his vertical industry and market knowledge (and that of his account team) as a way to increase relevance and value to C-level executives in the client organization. **AOE in Action:** He started by conducting research to learn more about how new country-level immigration regulations would affect his clients' global business, mobility, and operations. By understanding these new changes, the account team has been able to focus their sales strategy on how they can best help their clients efficiently address these new needs and requirements. By being able to engage customers in these types of broader business-level conversations, the account executive and his team have opened up new business development opportunities. **Business Results:** The overall result has been increased customer satisfaction and an increase of 16 percent in share of wallet in the account.
AOE 7 Sales Team Management Case 8	**Background:** A corporate sales manager oversees a multigenerational, virtual team of 14 outside and inside sales representatives supporting global accounts in a technology company. **AOE in Action:** After attending a coaching and pipeline management training program, the manager started making regular one-on-one calls with her team to coach them on a disciplined use and management of the sales pipeline. She also paired the sales reps together, based on factors including generational differences, technology fluency, and vertical industry knowledge, coaching them to be engaged in peer tutoring. **Business Results:** The results so far have been very positive. The manager has observed improvement in the shape and size of the pipeline and expects to see a higher win rate of high-quality opportunities in the coming months.

AOE 8 **Sales Coaching** **Case 9**	**Background:** An inside sales manager leads a team of 16 sales reps whose experience ranges from six months on the job to over 35 years in sales. **AOE in Action:** To help manage his team, the manager developed and implemented a new performance management approach. It included a performance review template that was simple, clear, and measurable so his sales reps knew what was expected not only from a sales perspective but also in terms of integrity, teamwork, and customer satisfaction. The manager also created weekly scorecards so that the reps could track themselves relative to those measures. To ensure the success of the newly created performance management approach, the sales manager defined and implemented a structured coaching approach. He started by creating an "individual coaching plan" (ICP) for each sales rep that captured his observations and concrete information about the strengths and opportunities for improvement. The ICP also included major coaching focus areas, planned activities, and a timeline for completing the activities. The manager scheduled biweekly coaching sessions to implement the ICP. During these coaching sessions, he provided concrete feedback on metrics and shared observations, created an open and honest environment to talk about specific and measurable steps that could be taken to improve performance, conducted role plays, and made necessary mid-course corrections to the ICP. **Business Results:** By setting clear expectations and providing consistent coaching and communication, the sales manager has seen positive impact on his team's morale and on their sales performance (11 percent year-over-year growth in quota attainment).
AOE 9 **Sales Talent** **Selection** **Case 10**	**Background:** A sales recruiter is in charge of attracting/finding, screening, and hiring candidates for a software company's inside sales call center. Recently, the company seemed to be experiencing higher than usual turnover with their inside sales reps. **AOE in Action:** To enhance employee retention, the sales recruiter met directly with the inside sales managers and team leaders to better understand their needs and requirements. The sales recruiter wanted to assess whether the current job description, level, and pay grade were reasonable and aligned to management expectations. One of the main job requirements had been prior call center experience, but there had been no clear differentiation between inside sales experience and customer support experience. Customer support and sales require very different skill sets. The reps who had not previously worked in a sales environment often lacked the basic sales skills as well as the entrepreneurial spirit and motivation required for job success. This difference in perspective, coupled with a challenging sales quota, often meant that new hires were quickly discouraged and left. The sales recruiter changed the job description and interview questions to focus more on sales-specific competencies. The result was that the sales recruiter was better able to target, recruit, and hire candidates who were motivated by the challenges and benefits of the sales organization and culture. **Business Results:** This change has increased employee retention (attrition rate has decreased by 9 percent) and saved the company money associated with employee turnover.

(continued)

Table 1-1: Case Examples Aligned to AOEs (continued)

AOE 10 **Sales Talent** **Development** **Case 11**	*Background:* A learning strategist in a global accounting and consulting firm is responsible for defining, designing, and evaluating sales talent development programs. *AOE in Action:* By using the analytics capability of the firm's customer relationship management (CRM) system to conduct win analysis for various sales teams, this individual has identified potential opportunities for sales skill development, used the insights gained to revise the sales methodology training program, and has also shared insights about individual teams with their sales team leaders to implement follow-up sales coaching efforts. *Business Results:* So far, the combination of revised sales methodology training and follow-up targeted coaching using real-world examples from the firm's sales pipeline has enhanced the relevance, efficiency, and effectiveness of its sales training. The learning strategist has also developed plans to evaluate the long-term business impact of the new program on metrics such as pipeline size, win rate, and quota attainment by using the same analytics that were applied to initially define the new program.
AOE 11 **Sales Tool** **and Process** **Improvement** **Case 12**	*Background:* A sales enablement organization was asked by its global sales leaders to simplify the company's quoting approval system. Global account managers (GAMs) were spending too much time chasing down approvals from country, regional, and global sales management to finalize their quotes. Customers and partners wanted a quick turnaround, but the existing system's lack of automation, coupled with time zone differences, was creating a major barrier. *AOE in Action:* A sales enablement specialist conducted a requirements analysis and then used the insights to create a blueprint for optimizing the system. The sales enablement team used the blueprint to enhance the system. The new system was more efficient for all parties. One simple but significant change included an automated alert system that lets GAMs know that approvals have been received and that lets partners know as soon as a quote has been approved. GAMs no longer have to "chase down" approvals, and partners can move forward on a deal without any delay. *Business Results:* Partners are finding it easier to do business with the organization, and the new system has had a significant overall impact on the sales organization, including increased productivity, accelerated deal closings, improved partner and customer satisfaction, and enhanced employee morale (less stress).
AOE 12 **Sales** **Incentive and** **Compensation** **Design** **Case 13**	*Background:* A sales compensation specialist was responsible for designing and implementing a new incentive and compensation plan for a small life sciences company. *AOE in Action:* The specialist made sure the new plan was aligned to the company's business objectives and used knowledge of the many factors involved in an incentive plan to make sure the package rewarded the right sales behaviors, accounted for variations in selling environments, and factored in metrics that affect the more qualitative elements of selling (for example, teamwork, flexibility, and initiative). The compensation specialist clearly communicated the performance metrics to the sales force and developed a monthly report to share individual and team results. The company also rolled out a new CRM integrated sales incentive management system that provided the sales reps with user-friendly dashboards calculating their sales incentive earnings. *Business Results:* The new compensation plan, tools, and metrics have helped reduce anxiety and ambiguity about the sales-performance expectations for the sales force.

Addressing Roles Across the Sales Ecosystem

Sales is a complex phenomenon. To use a famous phrase: "It takes a village" to create a successful sales practice, as a number of roles are involved in the sales ecosystem. The new ATD WCSCM, like its predecessor, covers all major roles, including customer-facing roles (for example, sales representative, account manager, sales specialist, presales consultant), sales management and leadership, and sales enablement (such as sales trainer, sales recruiter, sales compensation specialist, and sales operations specialist). For each sales role, the new model defines unique AOEs that include the skills, knowledge, and behaviors required for success.

Having a comprehensive competency model enables sales organizations to set consistent standards across the different roles and to use the model to build talent development and talent management solutions for all its members.

A New Architecture for Enhanced Usability

Because the original ATD WCSCM covered all major roles in the sales profession, one of the goals of the revision was to enhance the usability of the new model by making it easier for users to map specific AOEs to each role and to find the skills, knowledge, and behaviors needed for their success.

To achieve this goal, a three-part architecture was adopted for the new model by dividing sales roles into three groups—sales force (that is, customer-facing and quota-carrying roles), sales management and leadership, and sales enablement. All AOEs that are unique to each role cluster are grouped together, allowing sales professionals to easily navigate through the new model and find the AOEs that are unique to the role they are researching.

Table 1-2: How to Use the Model

Example	A sales partner (channel) account manager can look at the Sales Force part of the model and select AOE 4 (Partner Sales Support) to learn about the unique skills, knowledge, and behaviors that are critical for success in this role, while a sales recruiter can go to the Sales Enablement part of the model and select AOE 9 (Sales Talent Selection) to learn about the skills, knowledge, and behaviors that are critical for success in the role of a sales recruiter. Of course, all members of the sales ecosystem need the foundational competencies, and any member of the sales ecosystem can easily access that section, which is shared by all roles. Additionally, a general awareness of tangential AOEs is extremely helpful for professionals in the sales ecosystem. For example, it is very helpful for sales talent developers or sales recruiters to have an awareness of all AOEs for Sales Force and Sales Management & Leadership as they define, design, and develop learning solutions or as they attract, screen, and hire sales professionals.

Scalable to Sales Organizations of Various Sizes

The new model is designed to be applicable to sales organizations of various sizes and maturity levels. By grouping AOEs that are unique to a set of sales roles together, the three-part model is:

- beneficial to large sales organizations with highly differentiated roles
- beneficial to smaller sales organizations, where the roles are less differentiated and one person needs the required competencies to perform multiple tasks.

Table 1-3: Examples of Scalability of WCSCM

Example	The Sales Force part of the model includes AOEs unique to customer-facing and quota-carrying sales roles, such as sales representatives, presales consultants, and channel account managers. In sales organizations where these roles are differentiated, sales professionals can focus on AOEs unique to each specialized role. For example, presales consultants can focus on AOE 3 (Complex Solution Definition and Positioning), while a channel partner account manager can focus on AOE 4 (Partner Sales Support). On the other hand, in smaller sales organizations where one sales rep wears multiple hats, focus can be broadened to multiple AOEs to learn about needed skills, knowledge, and behaviors required for success in accomplishing the duties of this more wide-ranging role.

Adaptable and Capable of Being Contextualized

The new ATD WCSCM is focused at a generic level in order to be applicable to sale professionals in various industries worldwide. It provides sales organizations with a strong foundation and a starting point to customize the AOEs to fit the context of their industry and geography and the strategic priorities of their business by adding, removing, and/or modifying skills, knowledge, and behaviors in each AOE. For guidelines for customizing and adapting the new model to the context of your organization and your business needs, see chapter 8.

Limitations of the New ATD Sales Competency Model

It is worth noting that the new ATD sales competency model is, by design, somewhat limited in scope. For example, it does not describe the competencies needed by buyers to effectively engage sales professionals and collaborate with them to achieve win-win outcomes. The model does not focus on competencies unique to a specific industry, product or service type, or market segment. Furthermore, the new model does not describe different levels of proficiency within a competency. However, sales organizations that adopt the model can adapt it to identify and define different levels of proficiency for the behaviors tied to the competencies as a part of contextualization of the model to the type, objectives, and maturity level of their organizations. To address these limitations, in the future ATD might also create addendums to the WCSCM.

Research Methodology

In 2008, ATD used the results of a comprehensive study to create and publish the first WCSCM. Starting in the summer of 2014, ATD undertook another comprehensive research effort to revise and update the existing WCSCM, based on evolving trends and sales practices (Figure 1-1).

Figure 1-1: Overview of the Research Process

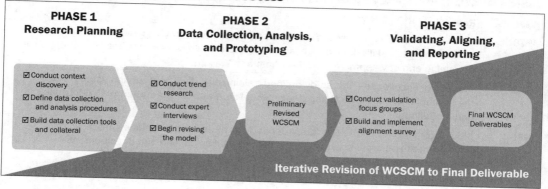

The research methodology involved an extensive exploration of evolving sales trends that are shaping the sales profession and influencing the competencies needed by sales professionals. These professionals include quota-carrying and customer-facing roles, sales management and leadership roles, and sales enablement roles (for example, sales recruiters, sales trainers and coaches, and professionals in sales compensation and sales operations).

The research continued with in-depth, one-on-one interviews with 59 thought leaders and leading sales practitioners worldwide in various industries to explore the evolving sales practices and their impacts on competencies needed by sales professionals today and in the foreseeable future. The results of interviews and the study of trends were used to revise the architecture and content of the 2008 sales competency model, producing the new model's 12 AOEs and four clusters of foundational competencies for sales professionals.

Validation data were collected on the new sales competency model through one-on-one reviews by thought leaders, focus group discussions with leading sales practitioners, and a large-scale survey with a wide range of sales and sales enablement practitioners and managers worldwide. A total of 295 sales professionals participated in the validation process. The results were used to prepare the new ATD World-Class Sales Competency Model.

This research methodology was similar to that used in 2007 to build the original sales competency model. Employing solid research methods to build a competency model is not new to ATD. The organization has a 35-year history of building research-based competency models and using them for a variety of talent development and talent management activities. Examples of these past efforts are shown in Table 1-4.

Table 1-4: ATD Competency Model Research Studies 1978–2013

Year	Report
1978	*A Study of Professional Training and Development Roles and Competencies*—This study defined the basic skills, knowledge, and other attributes required for effective performance of training and development activities (Pinto and Walker).
1983	*Models for Excellence*—This study defined training and development and established the format for all the ASTD Competency Model studies published since 1983 (McLagan and McCullough).
1989	*Models for HRD Practice*—This study defined the profession to include career development and organization development as well as training and development (McLagan and Suhadolnik).
1998	*ASTD Models for Learning Technologies: Roles, Competencies, and Outputs*—This study examined the roles, competencies, and work outputs that human resource development (HRD) professionals need to implement learning technologies in their organizations (Piskurich and Sanders).
1999	*ASTD Models for Human Performance Improvement: Roles, Competencies, and Outputs*—This study explored the roles, competencies, and outputs that human performance improvement professionals (or performance consultants) need in order to effect meaningful change within organizations (Rothwell).
1999	*ASTD Models for Workplace Learning and Performance*—This study explored what current and future competencies (five years beyond 1999) would be required to succeed in the field of Workplace Learning and Performance (Rothwell et al.).
2004	*ASTD Competency Study: Mapping the Future: Shaping New Workplace Learning and Performance Competencies*—This study strived to 1) identify the most significant trends and drivers that would impact current and future practice; 2) describe a comprehensive, inspiring, and future-oriented competency model; and 3) provide a foundation for competency-based applications, deliverables, and outputs—including certification (Bernthal et al.).
2009	*World-Class Selling: New Sales Competencies*—For enhanced sales team effectiveness, this book offers up-to-date criteria and data-driven documentation (B. Lambert, T. Ohai, and E.M. Kerkhoff).
2010	*Implementing the ATD World-Class Sales Competency Model: From Recommendation to Reality*—This study provides an overview of the sales competency model, the five levels of effectiveness, and sales-system maturity.
2013	*ASTD Competency Study: The Training & Development Profession Redefined*—The goal of this study was to update the knowledge, skills, abilities, and behaviors first identified in the 2004 study (Rothwell et al.).

Conclusion

Scalable to organizations of various sizes, the 2015 WCSCM model features business-essential and future-oriented competencies and provides sales organizations with a set of standards for achieving various sales talent management goals. The model is also adaptable through customization to various industries, geographies, and strategic priorities.

2

KEY TRENDS SHAPING THE SALES PROFESSION

Sales professionals strive to establish and nurture relationships with prospects and customers and to earn their trust in order to share insights and persuade them to take action and make a purchase decision. The world in which sales professionals operate, however, is constantly changing. Underlying drivers such as market dynamics and changing customer demands, demographic shifts, globalization, and disruptive technologies are fomenting a perfect storm of trends that are changing the context of how sellers and buyers interact with one another, how they share information, and how they make decisions.

Four Categories of Trends

A comprehensive study of trends and emerging sales practices led to the identification of 12 trends, which are grouped into four categories (Table 2-1).

Table 2-1: Trends Shaping the Sales Profession

I. Market Dynamics and Changing Customer Demands	II. Advances in Technology
1. Rise of Empowered Buyers 2. Sales Force Verticalization 3. Shift from "FAB" to "Solution" to "Insight" Selling 4. Blurring Lines Between Sales and Marketing 5. Adoption of a Hybrid Sales Model	6. On-Demand Availability 7. Omnipresent Social Media 8. Analytics-Based Prospecting **III. Workforce Reconfiguration** 9. Multigenerational Sales Teams and Customer Teams 10. Globalization of Teams and Customer Base **IV. Sales Talent Development** 11. Use of "Win" Analytics to Gain Learner Insights 12. Emergence of Integrated Learning Environments as a Necessity.

Category I: Market Dynamics and Changing Customer Demands

This category contains five trends that highlight the emergence of empowered buyers. These buyers expect sales teams to understand the dynamics of their vertical industry and have little interest in dealing with sales professionals who engage in transactional selling by citing product "feature, advantage, and benefit" (FAB). Instead, they are looking for a credible partner who has a solid understanding of their needs and who also challenges them, provides insights, and proposes customized and contextualized solutions to help them solve tomorrow's problems while helping them optimize and transform their current business.

This trend category also highlights a shift in traditional boundaries between functions (sales and marketing) and between organizational models (outside versus inside sales model), which has implications for sales talent development.

The five trends in this category and their implications for sales talent development are described in the following sections.

Trend 1: Rise of Empowered Buyers

The convergence of mobile, social, cloud, and big data innovations has ushered in an era of buyer empowerment. Today's tech-savvy customers, with access to a wider range of information sources, are better educated about available solutions than ever before. Most customers, in fact, prefer to conduct their own research by comparing product/service options, reading online reviews, and getting peer input through social media channels. Many customers are far advanced in the buying process before even engaging with a sales representative (Wesson 2014, Moore 2011, Porter 2013).

Implication. This trend calls for competencies in: 1) establishing a social media presence as a credible source of information for customers seeking to learn about trends, evolving solutions, and industry or market dynamics; 2) proactively researching and targeting prospects to initiate interest-building engagements on potential solutions for their evolving business needs and opportunities.

Trend 2: Sales Force Verticalization

Martin (2012) identifies verticalization of the sales force as a trend that parallels the growth of customer sophistication about purchased products and services and points to how these solutions fit into specific customer business strategies. Educated and empowered customers increasingly have a low tolerance for generic product/service information. They expect sales teams to understand the dynamics of their vertical industry, including its key performance indicators (KPIs) and the major challenges and opportunities that they and their competitors face.

Implication. This trend calls for competencies in 1) building vertical industry acumen; 2) articulating the unique value propositions of their proposed solutions, centered on the customer's unique needs in the context of industry KPIs.

Trend 3: Shift From "FAB" to "Solution" to "Insight" Selling

Today's buyers are less interested in dealing with sales professionals who engage in transactional selling by citing product FAB. Instead, they are looking for a credible partner who has a solid understanding of their needs and who also challenges them, provides insights, and proposes customized and contextualized solutions to help them solve tomorrow's problems while also helping them optimize and transform their current business. Adamson and Toman (2012) argue that the solution selling paradigm has shifted to insightful selling.

Implication. This trend calls for competencies in 1) using conventional and emerging research and analytics resources to gain an accurate understanding of the customer's needs and evolving challenges and opportunities; 2) challenging the customer's status quo and proposing solutions that take into account the customer's current and evolving needs and opportunities; 3) ensuring that solutions are justified, alternatives are explored, and best courses of action are articulated in the best interest of the customer.

Trend 4: Blurring Lines Between Sales and Marketing

Sales and marketing have traditionally been clearly delineated functions. Today, however, the lines between these two functions are becoming blurred. Resourceful and educated customers have access to the marketing messages and digital footprint of multiple solution providers. In most cases, they have begun to compare a variety of solutions before calling a sales representative. More and more, organizations are moving toward aligning and integrating their sales and marketing functions to ensure consistency in branding messages (Ledingham et al. 2014).

Implication. This trend calls for competencies in 1) using the organization's marketing and branding tools and resources to establish an accurate and enticing digital footprint in the marketplace; 2) collaborating with marketing colleagues to define and implement sales strategies and plans that engage with the right prospects, at the right stages of their buying process, and with the right blend of branding and sales value propositions.

Trend 5: Adoption of a Hybrid Sales Model

The continuing global economic downturn has pushed organizations to embrace a more cost-effective sales model; for example, by restricting corporate travel. The view that "face time" is always needed, particularly in large and global accounts, is being challenged (Davie et al. 2010). Customers are comfortable making decisions based on a mix of both face-to-face and virtual interactions. Furthermore, an increasing number of organizations are expanding and augmenting the traditional role of their inside sales representatives (ISRs). ISRs are no longer simply engaged in task substitution for the "feet-on-the-street" sales reps.

Implication. This trend calls for competencies in 1) enhancing fluency among sales professionals in the use of both conventional (phone, in-person meeting) and advanced virtual communication tools and technology (blogs, LinkedIn, Twitter, YouTube, Facebook, Pinterest); 2) augmenting competencies among ISRs to serve as "virtual sales specialists" and to participate fully in the end-to-end sales process.

Category II: Advances in Technology

This category highlights dramatic technological advances and their impacts on sales practices and required sales competencies. Examples include conventional and advanced mobile devices, the spread of social media as a major source of sales information for both buyers and sellers, and powerful pipeline and customer relationship management (CRM) technologies, along with big data mining and advanced analytics. The three trends in this category and their implications for sales talent development are described as follows:

Trend 6: On-Demand Availability

Conventional and advanced mobile devices (tablets, smartphones, and wearables) have contributed to on-demand availability and accessibility of both sellers and buyers. By providing on-demand voice, video, and text presence, this trend continues to reduce the need for exclusive in-person selling activities, while contributing to reduced cost and improved productivity of the sales force (Peacock 2012).

Implication. This trend calls for competencies in 1) adopting and using mobile devices and applications to extend presence, provide timely insights to customers, ensure responsiveness, respond to competitors' claims, and drive opportunities to close; 2) safeguarding against overuse and inappropriate use of mobile technology (for example, avoiding being intrusive to customers or creating technology fatigue and burnout for oneself).

Trend 7: Omnipresent Social Media

Social media is fast becoming a major source of sales information. Increasingly, buyers share their issues, concerns, requirements, and opinions on social media for all (including sales professionals) to see. Successful organizations and sales professionals make intelligent contributions to social communities and continually monitor their own presence on social media channels. What is said about a company on social media makes a difference to potential customers (Porter 2013, Wesson 2014).

Implication. This trend calls for competencies in 1) leveraging the intelligence from social media to engage potential customers in the right way, at the right time, and with the right message; 2) following key prospects in social media and providing timely insights to their information needs; 3) using social platforms to conduct real-time research and gain insight on customers and on the competition, using portable devices and applications.

Trend 8: Analytics-Based Prospecting

Powerful pipeline and CRM technologies and applications such as Salesforce.com, along with big-data mining and advanced analytics, are changing the way many sales organizations target and engage with customers. These organizations use data mining and advanced analytics to analyze customer data at a more granular level than with traditional approaches. They use intelligence gained from this analysis to obtain insights into customers' challenges, their past purchasing habits, what they value, and any untapped opportunities (Moritz et al. 2014, Ledingham et al. 2014).

Implication. This trend calls for competencies in 1) harnessing customers' digital footprint and CRM big data to gain actionable intelligence on customer priorities, needs, past purchases, and KPIs, as a way to synchronize planning and pursuit activities; 2) using customer intelligence and analytics to augment personal "intuitions" with accurate intelligence in prospecting and pursuit efforts.

Category III: Workforce Reconfiguration

This category highlights two trends: Both sales teams and customers are becoming multigenerational, and both the sales force and the customer base continue to become more globalized. The following is a description of the two trends in this category and their implications for sales talent development.

Trend 9: Multigenerational Sales Teams and Customer Teams

Both sales teams and the customer's purchasing teams are becoming multigenerational, with Millennials (born 1980 to 2000) becoming the dominant force as Baby Boomers (born 1946 to 1964) continue to retire, taking with them their experience-based wisdom. Millennials exhibit characteristics that make them uniquely different from preceding age groups. In terms of size, Millennials are now the largest generation across the globe (Schawbel 2012), and in 2015 Millennials became the majority demographic of the U.S. workforce, surpassing Generation X (those born between 1965 and 1980; Fry 2015).

Implication. This trend calls for competencies in 1) understanding generational differences and key characteristics of different generations (for example, adeptness with technology, motivating influences, work habits); 2) building and incorporating the tactics essential for working effectively with generational differences, especially when working with multigenerational purchasing teams at the customer organization.

Trend 10: Globalization of Teams and Customer Base

Continued globalization, accelerated by the interconnectedness of the world economy and by advances in virtual communication technologies, has created global sales teams and global customer purchasing teams, in which decisions are made in a distributed but unified manner, especially in global companies (Goldman and Kelly 2014).

Implication. This trend calls for competencies in 1) incorporating a global perspective in sales planning and pursuit efforts to accommodate multinational customer decision makers in multiple locations around the world, by being sensitive to local considerations (such as culture, law, rules, and regulations); 2) utilizing appropriate communication style and language to suit cultural, social, and linguistic differences so that any message is delivered correctly and professionally.

Category IV: Sales Talent Development

This category covers trends in sales force talent development, including the use of big data and analytics to extract valuable insights into the development needs of the sales team, as well as the emergence of learning environments as a business necessity. The two trends in this category and their implications for sales talent development are described in the following sections.

Trend 11: Use of "Win" Analytics to Gain Learner Insights

Today's advanced CRM systems and web-analytics tools capture information in unprecedented detail on sales successes and win challenges. Once mined, this granular data offers valuable insights into the development needs of the sales team and can be used to target desired behaviors and learning needs of individuals or teams, thereby remedying poor opportunity qualification, partnering issues, weak account planning, lack of timely follow-up, or poor call-to-close ratio (Russo 2014).

Implication. Sales talent developers need the following competencies 1) using win analytics and modeling techniques to assess the performance and learning needs of the sales force; 2) using the insight gained to adopt personalized, targeted, timely, engaging, and efficient learning and development (L&D) opportunities for sales team members.

Trend 12: Emergence of Integrated Learning Environments as a Necessity

The concept of learning environments is not new, but it is gaining momentum as a necessity to better accommodate rapidly shifting business needs, the growing virtualization and mobility of the sales force, and the learning preferences of Millennials (Verazi 2010; Elmgren 2013).

Implication. Sales talent developers need to expand their focus from "learning products" to fully integrated learning environments that embrace formal, informal, and social learning (for example, blogs and collaboration or community platforms). These emerging learning environments, which are more responsive to the sales force's preferences, content attributes, and on-demand need for learning, provide learning strategies such as 1) gamification—use of game technologies and attributes, such as Hoopla, LevelEleven, and Nitro, for the sales force to perform selling role plays in a virtual sales world; 2) technology-enabled crowd learning—the collaborative use of peer knowledge in real time; 3) learning videos—succinct vignettes that demonstrate the essence of a sales practice; 4) optimized mobile learning—use of various devices (such as tablets and smartphones) and delivery strategies (peer tutoring, learning portals, and Yammer groups) to give the sales force the freedom to structure their learning path.

Conclusion

Each of the trends discussed in this chapter has the potential to push a sales organization off course, but together they can create a perfect storm, requiring organizations to rethink their sales talent development practices. To stay on course and navigate the future, organizations need to adopt a multifaceted strategy to attract, select, engage, assess, retain, and continuously develop competent multigenerational global sales teams. These sales teams must be capable of interacting effectively with tech-savvy, educated, and demanding multigenerational global customers who are far advanced in their buying process when they engage sales teams.

Watch for these trends to continue to affect the way companies structure and restructure their sales and marketing organizations, make investment decisions in sales tools and processes, adopt new sales practices, and recruit, select, hire, and develop sales talent. The new WCSCM is designed to accommodate these trends and to assist organizations in using them to their advantage.

3

OVERVIEW OF THE NEW ATD WCSCM

This chapter describes the structure of the new World-Class Sales Competency Model (WCSCM) and the reasons for changing the structure of the original (2008) model. It details the roles that the new model includes and compares the areas of expertise (AOEs) and foundational competencies of the two models.

Comparison With the 2008 WCSCM

The 2008 ATD WCSCM used a pyramid image to illustrate the architecture of the model. The six categories of sales roles are placed at the top of the pyramid, all 13 AOEs are placed together in the middle, and the four clusters of foundational competencies form the base of the pyramid (Figure 3-1).

The results of interviews with leading sales practitioners in the 2014 study, as well as the feedback received by ATD over the past few years from end users of the model, indicated the need to simplify the model and enhance its usability by aligning the AOEs with specific roles in the sales profession.

To enhance the usability of the new model, making it easier for end users to locate the AOEs that are unique to each role and quickly find the descriptions of the skills, knowledge, and actions needed for success in the role, a three-part architecture was adopted. This architecture groups sales roles into three categories (instead of the six categories used in the original model) and uses more authentic role category titles (Table 3-1). Role category titles in the original model were more about different "hats" (for example, analyst, strategist, and consultant) that a sales professional wears within a role (such as sales account manager or sales manager). In contrast, the new role category titles are more closely aligned to job functions/categories (for example, sales force, sales management, and sales enablement). It also aligns and places AOEs for each role category together. The 12 sales AOEs are aligned with the three role categories. As in the original model, the foundational competencies that are shared by all role categories are placed at the base of the new model.

Figure 3-1: Architecture of the 2008 ATD WCSCM

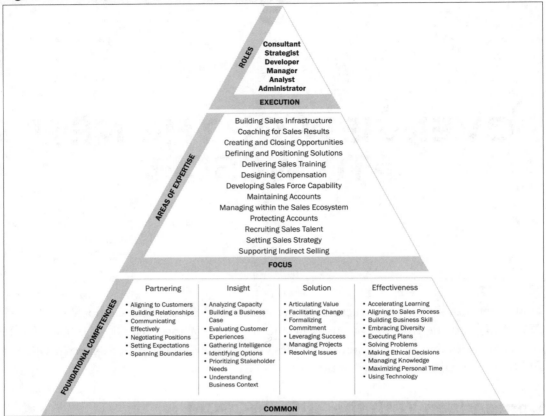

Table 3-1: Comparison of Role Categories in Original and New WCSCM

Original WCSCM Roles	New WCSCM Roles
• Consultant • Strategist • Developer • Manager • Analyst • Administrator	• Sales Force • Sales Management and Leadership • Sales Enablement

Role Categories in the New WCSCM

Similar to the 2008 model, the new ATD WCSCM covers all roles in the sales ecosystem; however, in the new model, these roles are grouped into three categories based on the manner of work performed: Sales Force, Sales Management and Leadership, and Sales Enablement (Table 3-2).

Table 3-2: Key Roles Covered in the New ATD WCSCM

Sales Force	Sales Enablement

• Sales representative:
  ○ Account manager
  ○ Territory manager
  ○ Account executive
• Inside/outside sales representative
• Sales specialist
• Presales technical consultant
• Partner/channel account manager
 	
Sales Management and Leadership
• Sales executive
• Sales manager
• Sales specialist manager
• Presales manager
• Partner/channel sales manager
	• Sales enablement individual contributors:
	  ○ Sales recruiter
	  ○ Sales compensation planner
	  ○ Sales technology specialist
	  ○ Sales operations analyst
	  ○ Sales trainer:
	    › Sales trainer/coach/consultant
	    › Sales training designer and developer
	  ○ Sales researcher
	  ○ Sales professor/academic
	• Sales enablement manager
	• Sales enablement executive

Sales Force

This role category consists of customer-facing sales professionals who are directly responsible for generating revenue and who usually carry quota. They are engaged in acquiring, developing, and retaining accounts, identifying and qualifying opportunities, defining and positioning solutions, selling with and through partners, and managing and advancing the sales pipeline. This category consists of the following roles:

Sales Representative

Sales professionals in this role serve as the sales lead for an account and work with clients to understand their needs and requirements, striving to provide them with solutions that fulfill these requirements. Typical job tiles within this role are account manager, territory account manager, account executive, and inside and outside sales representative. Sales professionals in this role are typically responsible for:

- driving business value for the client, while maximizing competitive share, revenue, and margin for the company
- identifying, qualifying, and pursing sales opportunities
- representing the company's portfolio of products and services and highlighting the company's key competitive advantages
- coordinating the overall account management activities with various businesses and functions within the company and managing and motivating support teams and resources to achieve sales results
- achieving sales goals independently or with presales, sales specialist, and partner sales.

Sales Specialist

Sales professionals in this role, compared to sales representatives, have specialized knowledge about products, services, and solutions offered by the company. Typical job titles within this role are sales consultant; product, service, or solution specialist; or solution generalist. Sales specialists are typically responsible for:

- leading pursuit in their assigned area of specialization
- collaborating with and supporting account managers, as well as providing specialist expertise within the sales team
- driving sales campaigns in their area of specialization to build the pipeline
- supporting sales representatives to qualify, negotiate, and close opportunities in their area of specialization.

Presales Technical Consultant

Designes, ecomplte, RTL

Sales professionals in this role possess an in-depth knowledge of both the company's and competitors' solutions and are engaged in technical selling. Typical job titles in this role are technology strategist, account technologist, and solution architect. Presales technical consultants are typically responsible for:

- working with the customer to define technical requirements and architect solutions, as well as prepare design specifications and other technical components of the proposals
- collaborating with sales teams to support the sales of complex solutions
- providing technical consulting to customers and account teams during the pursuit process
- giving technical support in sales proposals, presentations, product demonstrations, and customer enablement activities.

Partner/Channel Account Manager

Dealer Support

Sales professionals in this role ensure the success of the indirect sales motion of the company by establishing and nurturing relationships with channel partners. Typical job titles in this role are reseller partner account manager, distribution partner account manager, retail account manager, retail territory manager, and partner sales specialist. Partner/channel account managers are responsible for:

- establishing mutually beneficial relationships with partners (such as retailers, resellers, and distributors) to drive additional revenue with joint sales efforts
- acting as a focal point for all activities with the partner, including education, marketing, executive briefings, business planning, and end-user customer engagements
- acting as a liaison between partners and the company to ensure achievement of mutually beneficial outcomes
- managing execution of joint business plans (JBPs) with partners.

Sales Management and Leadership

TS Dirs, Sales Dir, GA Dirs

This role category consists of sales professionals who are engaged in setting and executing sales strategies, coaching and managing high-performing sales teams, and managing sales forecasts and achievement of revenue goals. Sales managers and leaders are responsible for:

- managing a group of sales professionals in one or more of the sales functions (account management, territory sales, specialties, inside sales, and presales)

- setting the direction and managing the deliverables of the assigned sales team, as well as achieving revenue and expense objectives
- resolving customer problems and participating in important negotiations with key customers
- building strategic executive relationships externally with clients and internally with company executives
- partnering with internal and external resources to develop best-in-class solutions for customers
- managing the performance of sales teams and their individual members
- coaching and developing sales talent within the organization.

Typical sales roles within this role category include:

- **Sales executive**—Senior-level sales manager who oversees the sales organization and associated resources
- **Sales manager**—Supervisor of customer-facing sales representatives
- **Sales specialist manager**—Supervisor of customer-facing sales teams with specialization in selling specific products, services, or solutions
- **Presales manager**—Supervisor of very technical sales teams who are engaged in defining complex solutions, creating proofs of concept, or prototyping complex solutions
- **Partner/channel sales manager**—Supervisor of those who manage relationships with the indirect sales force.

Sales Enablement

This role category consists of sales professionals who are not customer facing and are engaged in an ongoing process of recruiting, selecting, hiring, onboarding, developing, equipping, motivating, and rewarding the sales force and sales management to achieve business results. This category consists of a variety of roles spread over a number of functions within organizations, such as human resources, training and talent development, sales operations, and information technology. Depending on the size and maturity of the company, these professionals might reside in these functions while they are supporting the sales organization in a part- or full-time capacity. Regardless of their organizational affiliation, sales enablement professionals are responsible for:

- attracting, recruiting, selecting, and onboarding winning sales teams
- defining, designing, developing, acquiring, and deploying learning and information-sharing solutions to continuously develop sales talent
- determining, implementing, and constantly fine-tuning reward and compensation systems to motivate the sales team to achieve the strategic objectives of the organization
- equipping the sales force with the tools, processes, and support needed to
  - gain customer and competitor intelligence
  - provide potential buyers and current customers with valuable insights
  - capture, track, and move opportunities to closure.
- providing the needed support to enhance the productivity of the sales teams.

Typical roles in this role category include:

- sales recruiter
- sales compensation planner
- sales technology specialist
- sales operations analyst
- sales trainer:
  - sales trainer/coach/consultant (sales instructor, facilitator, sales consultant, sales coach)
  - sales training designer and developer
  - sales talent developer
- sales researcher
- sales professor/academic
- sales enablement manager
  - operations manager
  - compensation manager
  - recruitment manager
- sales enablement executive
  - director or vice president of sales operations
  - director or vice president of compensation
  - director or vice president of sales training and talent development
  - chief learning officer.

Architecture of the New WCSCM

The major change in the new model—the organization of new and revised AOEs into three sales groups—creates an architecture that enhances usability and makes it easier for users to quickly locate and use information (Figure 3-2).

Figure 3-2: Architecture of the New ATD Three-Part WCSCM

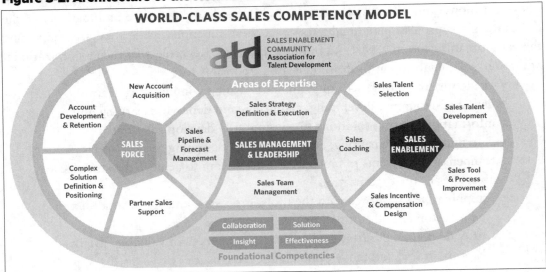

Each sales group in the model—Sales Force, Sales Management and Leadership, and Sales Enablement—contains specific AOEs, and there are two AOEs shared by two groups. The three sales groups are described as follows:

Sales Force

This part of the model focuses on quota-carrying, customer-facing sales professionals. The following five AOEs are aligned to Sales Force roles:

- AOE 1: New Account Acquisition
- AOE 2: Account Development and Retention
- AOE 3: Complex Solution Definition and Positioning
- AOE 4: Partner Sales Support
- AOE 5: Sales Pipeline and Forecast Management *(shared with Sales Management and Leadership)*.

Sales Management and Leadership

This part of the model focuses on sales professionals who are engaged in setting and executing sales strategies and in coaching and managing high-performing sales teams. Four AOEs are aligned to Sales Management and Leadership—two AOEs are unique, one is shared with Sales Force, and one is shared with Sales Enablement:

- AOE 5: Sales Pipeline and Forecast Management *(shared with Sales Force)*
- AOE 6: Sales Strategy Definition and Execution
- AOE 7: Sales Team Management
- AOE 8: Sales Coaching *(shared with Sales Enablement)*.

Sales Enablement

This part of the model focuses on sales enablement professionals who are engaged in attracting, recruiting, selecting, hiring, onboarding, developing, assessing, equipping, motivating, and rewarding members of the sales force and sales management to achieve business results. Roles include sales trainers, sales recruiters, sales operations, and sales compensation. The following AOEs are aligned to sales enablement professionals:

- AOE 8: Sales Coaching *(shared with Sales Management and Leadership)*
- AOE 9: Sales Talent Selection
- AOE 10: Sales Talent Development
- AOE 11: Sales Tool and Process Improvement
- AOE 12: Sales Incentive and Compensation Design.

Note: For more detailed descriptions of AOEs and insights from the validation survey about their relative importance for various roles, see chapter 4.

Comparison of the Original and New AOEs

The original model contained 13 AOEs, which were examined and revised in light of research findings. The scope of revision varied depending on the AOE. Some were slightly revised, some were substantially changed, and some were incorporated into a new AOE (Table 3-3).

Table 3-3: Comparison of the Original and New AOEs

Original Model AOEs	Notes on Revision	New Model AOEs
1. Creating and Closing Opportunities	Revised these three original AOEs and adopted the value chain of Acquisition, Development, and Retention to create two new AOEs that differentiate account acquisition or hunting practices (including creating and closing opportunities) from sales farming practices targeted for account expansion and retention.	**New Account Acquisition (AOE 1)**
2. Protecting Accounts		**Account Development and Retention (AOE 2)**
3. Maintaining Accounts		
4. Defining and Positioning Solutions	Title modification addresses the portfolio knowledge and value proposition that is increasingly required in value selling (versus price-point transactional sales). Also addresses technical and complex solution selling and insight selling practices.	**Complex Solution Definition and Positioning (AOE 3)**
5. Supporting Indirect Selling	Title modification to enhance usability. The content was also updated to enhance partner support through advanced analytics and more structured partner business planning.	**Partner Sales Support (AOE 4)**
6. Note: The original model did not include a dedicated AOE in this area.	New AOE based on research that brings out the increasingly critical role of customer relationship management (CRM) and associated sales force responsibilities for managing and tracking sales data to ensure accurate and reliable business intelligence.	**Sales Pipeline and Forecast Management (AOE 5)**
7. Setting Sales Strategy	Changed the content of the original AOE to bring out balanced risk taking and management, as well as profit-and-loss ownership or support.	**Sales Strategy Definition and Execution (AOE 6)**
8. Managing Within the Sales Ecosystem	Changed the title and sharpened the focus on management of sales teams.	**Sales Team Management (AOE 7)**
9. Coaching for Sales Results	More emphasis in the content on intergenerational differences that require alternative coaching strategies to maintain continuity of performance.	**Sales Coaching (AOE 8)**
10. Recruiting Sales Talent	Title modification to enhance usability. Content was also enhanced to use social media and advanced technologies to recruit and build a solid talent pipeline.	**Sales Talent Selection (AOE 9)**

Original Model AOEs	Notes on Revision	New Model AOEs
11. Delivering Sales Training Developing Sales Force Capability	*Based on research, the merging of previous AOEs recognizes the need for advanced analytics to define learning needs and for using a blended learning approach, more self-directed learning in the field, and the harnessing of technology and new learning practices (e.g., webinars, games, blogs, peer-to-peer knowledge transfer).*	**Sales Talent Development (AOE 10)**
12. Building Sales Infrastructure	*Title modification to enhance usability. Content enhanced to identify accelerating use of innovative technology (e.g., social media, CRM, mobile connectivity, big data) in capturing and managing sales data, preparing for and pursuing opportunities, and facilitating knowledge transfer.*	**Sales Tool and Process Improvement (AOE 11)**
13. Designing Compensation	*Title modification to enhance usability. Content enhanced to leverage multifaceted strategy conducive to the needs of a changing sales force.*	**Sales Incentive and Compensation Design (AOE 12)**

Comparison of the Original and New Foundational Competencies

This section of the model—shared by all sales professionals—consists of four clusters of competencies, which have been modified from the original WCSCM (Table 3-4). The four clusters are described as follows:

Collaboration

These competencies enable sales professionals to interact and work interdependently with others. Examples include relationship building, alignment building, strategic partnering, and teaming.

Insight

Through skills in information analysis and synthesis, these competencies enable sales professionals to develop a robust understanding of their customers and to use this insight to facilitate and guide customer decision making. Examples include business and financial acumen, sector/industry insight, and research/analysis.

Solution

These competencies enable sales professionals to develop strategies for identifying the right solution to customers' complex problems, generating enthusiasm for the solution they propose, competitively positioning the solution, and negotiating and gaining commitment. Examples include product/service acumen, competitive intelligence, consultative insight, and complex problem solving.

Effectiveness

By demonstrating personal and professional effectiveness and responsibility, these competencies enable sales professionals to deal with accelerating change and the dynamic nature of the sales environment. Examples include global awareness, diversity and multigenerational effectiveness, sales process acumen, technology fluency, and ethical decision making.

Note: For more detailed descriptions of the foundational competencies and insights from the validation survey about their relative importance, see chapter 5.

Table 3-4: Comparison of Original and New Foundational Competencies

Original Model Title	Description of Changes	New Model Title
1. Spanning Boundaries	*New title; expanded*	**Alignment Building**
2. Communicating Effectively	*New title; sharpened*	**Effective Communication**
3. Aligning to Customers	*New title; sharpened*	**Customer Advocacy**
4. Setting Expectations	*Removed; content incorporated into Negotiating and Gaining Commitment*	
5. Negotiating Positions	*New title; expanded*	**Negotiating and Gaining Commitment**
6. Building Relationships	*New title; sharpened*	**Relationship Building**
	New Competency	**Strategic Partnering**
	New Competency	**Teaming**
	New Competency	**Transformational Leadership**
7. Analyzing Capacity	*Removed*	
8. Evaluating Customer Experiences	*Sharpened*	**Evaluating Customer Experiences**
9. Gathering Intelligence	*Removed; content incorporated into Research/Analysis*	
10. Prioritizing Stakeholder Needs	*Removed; content incorporated into Consultative Insight*	
11. Identifying Options	*Removed; content incorporated into Consultative Insight*	
12. Understanding Business Context 13. Building a Business Case 14. Building Business Skill	*Collapsed multiple competencies into a newly titled and crisper competency*	**Business and Financial Acumen**
	Added new competency	**Competitive Intelligence**
	Added new competency	**Product/Service Acumen**
	Added new competency	**Sector/Industry Insight**
	Added new competency	**Consultative Insight**
	Added new competency	**Research/Analysis**

Original Model Title	Description of Changes	New Model Title
15. Facilitating Change	*Removed; content incorporated into Project Management*	
16. Formalizing Agreements	*Removed; content incorporated into Negotiating and Gaining Commitment*	
17. Resolving Issues	*Removed; content incorporated into Negotiating and Gaining Commitment*	
18. Managing Projects	*New title; content expanded*	**Project Management**
19. Leveraging Success	*Removed; content incorporated into Strategic Partnering*	
20. Articulating Value	*Removed; content incorporated into Consultative Insight*	
21. Solving Problems	*New title; sharpened*	**Complex Problem Solving**
22. Embracing Diversity	*New title; content expanded*	**Diversity Effectiveness**
	Added new competency	**Multigenerational Effectiveness**
	Added new competency	**Global Awareness**
23. Making Ethical Decisions	*New title*	**Ethical Decision Making**
24. Managing Knowledge	*Removed*	
25. Using Technology	*New title; sharpened*	**Technology Fluency**
26. Accelerating Learning	*Removed*	
27. Executing Plans	*Removed*	
28. Maximizing Personal Time	*Removed*	
29. Aligning to Sales Processes	*New title; simplified*	**Sales Process Acumen**

Conclusion

This chapter provided an overview of the new ATD WCSCM, describing the rationale behind the structure of the new model and presenting a side-by-side comparison of the new AOEs and foundational competencies with those in the original (2008) model. The next two chapters provide detailed descriptions of the AOEs and foundational competencies and share highlights from a survey of sales professionals about their relative importance on the job.

4

AREAS OF EXPERTISE

Twelve areas of expertise (AOEs) are defined in the new ATD World-Class Sales Competency Model (WCSCM). These AOEs are grouped together and aligned to the three major role categories (Sales Force, Sales Management and Leadership, and Sales Enablement) in the sales ecosystem. Each AOE consists of four components:

- **key knowledge areas**—various knowledge areas that are critical to successful performance on the job
- **key skills**—critical skills needed to perform various tasks related to the AOE
- **key actions**—observable behaviors and activities required for effective performance in the AOE
- **sample outputs**—examples of tangible outcomes produced by sales professionals in the AOE.

During the validation phase of the study, the key knowledge, skills, and actions for each AOE were validated by thought leaders and leading practitioners in one-on-one review sessions and focus groups and by respondents to the validation survey.

This chapter presents descriptions of the AOEs aligned to the three parts of the new model and offers key survey findings about these AOEs. For more detailed descriptions of the key knowledge, skills, actions, and sample outputs for these AOEs, see Appendix A. For detailed results of the validation survey, see Appendix D.

AOEs Aligned to the Sales Force

This part of the model focuses on quota-carrying, customer-facing sales professionals who are engaged in acquiring, developing, and retaining accounts; defining and positioning complex solutions; selling with and through partners; and managing and advancing the sales pipeline. Roles include account managers, inside and outside sales representatives, sales specialists, presales consultants, and partner/channel sales representatives (Figure 4-1). A description follows of the five AOEs aligned to Sales Force.

Figure 4-1: AOEs Aligned to Sales Force

AOE 1: New Account Acquisition

This AOE includes knowledge, skills, and actions required to pursue opportunities and acquire new accounts by:

- identifying and qualifying opportunities
- researching prospects
- identifying and prioritizing prospect needs
- aligning value propositions with business and personal needs and key performance indicators (KPIs) of prospects
- proposing and competitively positioning solutions
- negotiating and gaining customer commitment.

AOE 2: Account Development and Retention

This AOE includes the knowledge, skills, and actions required to nurture, grow, and maintain existing accounts by:

- monitoring, measuring, and ensuring customer satisfaction
- leveraging existing contracts for up-selling and cross-selling opportunities
- actively troubleshooting and resolving issues
- countering competitive threats
- expanding customer networks and champions.

AOE 3: Complex Solution Definition and Positioning

This AOE includes the knowledge, skills, and actions required to drive or support complex sales opportunities by:

- translating business requirements into technical solution requirements
- coordinating technical expertise
- sizing, scoping, and defining delivery and deployment approach and timeline

- identifying required resources
- coordinating demonstrations and proof of concept
- supporting internal deal acceptance.

AOE 4: Partner Sales Support

This AOE includes the knowledge, skills, and actions required to manage and support indirect (channel) selling by:

- preparing joint business and marketing plans
- co-selling with partners
- onboarding and training partners on the company's strategies and priorities, products and solutions, and partner incentive programs
- advocating for partners internally and protecting their interests.

AOE 5: Sales Pipeline and Forecast Management *(shared with Sales Management and Leadership)*

This AOE includes the knowledge, skills, and actions required to use the sales process to manage sales opportunities, leverage the power of sales analytics to exploit sales opportunities, and ensure achievement of business results by:

- populating and managing the sales pipeline
- managing and protecting margin
- developing and monitoring sales forecasts
- utilizing customer relationship management (CRM) systems.

Most Important AOEs for Sales Force

In the validation phase of the study, participants in Sales Force roles were asked to rate the importance of AOEs to their success on the job, using a 5-point scale (with 5 being critical) (See Table 4-1 for the proportion of survey respondents who provided ratings of 4 or 5.) The following four AOEs were identified as most important:

- Complex Solution Definition and Positioning
- New Account Acquisition
- Account Development and Retention
- Sales Pipeline and Forecast Management.

Table 4-1: Most Important AOEs for Sales Force

AOE	Area of Expertise	Importance %
1	Complex Solution Definition and Positioning	80%
2	Account Development and Retention	78%
3	New Account Acquisition	78%
4	Sales Pipeline and Forecast Management	78%
5	Sales Strategy Definition and Execution	60%

(continued)

Table 4-1: Most Important AOEs for Sales Force (continued)

AOE	Area of Expertise	Importance %
6	Sales Tool and Process Improvement	43%
7	Partner Sales Support	40%
8	Sales Coaching	40%
9	Sales Talent Development	35%
10	Sales Talent Selection	35%
11	Sales Team Management	35%
12	Sales Incentive and Compensation Design	23%

Where Sales Force Spends Most Time

Participants in the Sales Force roles were also asked to select the top three AOEs where they spend most of their time (Table 4-2). The highest percentage of participants identified the following AOEs:

- Complex Solution Definition and Positioning
- Account Development and Retention
- New Account Acquisition.

Table 4-2: Where Sales Force Spends Most Time

AOE	Area of Expertise	Time spent %
1	Complex Solution Definition and Positioning	68%
2	Account Development and Retention	65%
3	New Account Acquistion	63%
4	Sales Pipeline and Forecast Management	25%
5	Sales Strategy Definition and Execution	25%
6	Partner Sales Support	13%
7	Sales Talent Development	13%
8	Sales Tool and Process Improvement	10%
9	Sales Coaching	8%
10	Sales Team Management	13%
11	Sales Incentive and Compensation Design	0%
12	Sales Talent Selection	0%

AOEs Aligned to Sales Management and Leadership

This part of the model focuses on sales professionals who need skills and knowledge in setting and executing sales strategies, coaching and managing high-performing sales teams, and managing sales forecasts. Roles include sales managers, presales managers, partner/channel sales managers, sales directors, and sales executives. The Sales Management and Leadership part consists of four AOEs—two AOEs are unique, one is shared with Sales Force, and one is shared with Sales Enablement (Figure 4-2). A description follows of the four AOEs aligned to Sales Management and Leadership roles.

Figure 4-2: AOEs Aligned to Sales Management and Leadership

AOE 5: Sales Pipeline and Forecast Management *(shared with Sales Force)*

This AOE includes the knowledge, skills, and actions required to use the sales process to manage sales opportunities, leverage the power of sales analytics to exploit sales opportunities, and ensure achievement of business results by:

- populating and managing the sales pipeline
- managing and protecting margin
- developing and monitoring sales forecasts
- using CRM systems.

AOE 6: Sales Strategy Definition and Execution

This AOE includes the knowledge, skills, and actions required to develop and implement sales strategies appropriate to market segments and customer-unique needs by:

- monitoring emerging market trends
- setting the priorities, direction, and framework for more tactical sales planning
- ensuring internal organizational buy-in
- leveraging innovative sales practices and automated sales tools
- translating the sales strategy to actionable plans and courses of action
- empowering the team to execute the strategy
- setting metrics to measure success.

AOE 7: Sales Team Management

This AOE includes the knowledge, skills, and actions required to manage sales teams effectively by:

- analyzing sales team data (such as forecasts and progress to goals)
- ensuring achievement of metrics (such as quota and margin attainment)
- allocating resources and managing budgets

- attracting, selecting, onboarding, developing, coaching, motivating, promoting, and terminating personnel
- conducting performance reviews and career planning
- removing demotivating factors in the environment and enhancing collective team competencies.

AOE 8: Sales Coaching *(shared with Sales Enablement)*

This AOE includes the knowledge, skills, and actions required to use sales coaching to develop sales teams and drive sales effectiveness by:

- providing the structured guidance essential for developing sellers
- setting clear performance expectations linked to business metrics
- developing individualized coaching plans
- observing and targeting performance gaps
- providing on-the-job reinforcement and corrective feedback
- modeling expected behaviors.

Most Important AOEs for Sales Management and Leadership

In the validation phase of the study, participants in the Sales Management and Leadership roles were asked to rate the importance of the AOEs to their success on the job using a 5-point scale (with 5 being critical). The following six AOEs were identified as most important. (See Table 4-3 for the proportion of survey respondents who provided ratings of 4 or 5.)

- Account Development and Retention
- New Account Acquisition
- Complex Solution Definition and Positioning
- Sales Strategy Definition and Execution
- Sales Talent Development
- Sales Coaching.

Table 4-3: Most Important AOEs for Sales Management and Leadership

AOE	Area of Expertise	Importance %
1	Account Development and Retention	96%
2	Complex Solution Definition and Positioning	90%
3	New Account Acquistion	90%
4	Sales Strategy Definition and Execution	88%
5	Sales Talent Development	88%
6	Sales Coaching	85%
7	Sales Team Management	79%
8	Sales Talent Selection	77%
9	Sales Pipeline and Forecast Management	73%
10	Sales Tool and Process Improvement	67%
11	Partner Sales Support	60%
12	Sales Incentive and Compensation Design	58%

Where Sales Management and Leadership Personnel Spend Most Time

Participants in the Sales Management and Leadership roles were also asked to select the top three AOEs where they spend the most time. (See Table 4-4 for the proportion of survey respondents who provided ratings of 4 or 5.) The highest percentage of participants identified the following AOEs:

- New Account Acquisition
- Account Development and Retention
- Complex Solution Definition and Positioning
- Sales Strategy Definition and Execution
- Sales Coaching.

These study responses indicate that many managers spend more time selling and performing administrative tasks than they do coaching, managing their teams, and forecasting and managing the sales pipeline.

Table 4-4: Where Sales Management and Leadership Personnel Spend Most Time

AOE	Area of Expertise	Time Spent %
1	New Account Acquisition	54%
2	Account Development and Retention	38%
3	Complex Solution Definition and Positioning	38%
4	Sales Strategy Definition and Execution	38%
5	Sales Coaching	37%
6	Sales Talent Development	27%
7	Sales Team Management	27%
8	Sales Pipeline and Forecast Management	12%
9	Sales Tool and Process Improvement	12%
10	Partner Sales Support	10%
11	Sales Talent Selection	4%
12	Sales Incentive and Compensation Design	0%

AOEs Aligned to Sales Enablement

This part of the model focuses on sales enablement professionals, who need skills and knowledge in attracting, selecting, onboarding, developing, equipping, motivating, rewarding, and retaining the personnel in Sales Force and in Sales Management and Leadership to achieve business results. Roles include sales trainers, sales recruiters, sales operations, and sales compensation (Figure 4-3). A description follows of the five AOEs aligned to Sales Enablement roles.

Figure 4-3: AOEs Aligned to Sales Enablement

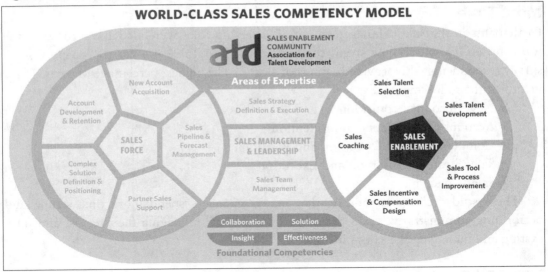

AOE 8: Sales Coaching *(shared with Sales Management and Leadership)*

This AOE includes the knowledge, skills, and actions required to use sales coaching to develop sales teams and drive sales effectiveness by:

- providing the structured guidance essential for developing sellers
- setting clear performance expectations linked to business metrics
- developing individualized coaching plans
- observing and targeting performance gaps
- providing on-the-job reinforcement and corrective feedback
- modeling expected behaviors.

AOE 9: Sales Talent Selection

This AOE includes the knowledge, skills, and actions required to recruit, screen, and hire sales talent by:

- building accurate job descriptions
- establishing performance and financial expectations with candidates
- collaborating with hiring agencies to recruit the right candidates
- managing negotiations with candidates
- supporting the smooth transition of new hires into the organization.

AOE 10: Sales Talent Development

This AOE includes the knowledge, skills, and actions required to develop a high-performing sales team by:

- assessing talent development needs
- creating or acquiring learning solutions
- delivering and deploying sales training

- offering knowledge management opportunities
- measuring and evaluating the impact of learning and development solutions
- managing or supporting learning management systems
- defining and implementing learning road maps tailored to individual and role-based career paths.

AOE 11: Sales Tool and Process Improvement

This AOE includes the knowledge, skills, and actions required to ensure availability of effective sales tools and processes by:

- defining, acquiring, and managing sales processes, tools, and systems
- incorporating emerging or advanced sales automation in support of business analytics, mobility, and CRM
- maintaining process, tool, or system usability and integrity.

AOE 12: Sales Incentive and Compensation Design

This AOE includes the knowledge, skills, and actions required to create and maintain equitable sales compensation and incentive practices, to ensure a motivated sales force by:

- researching industry sales compensation metrics
- ensuring that compensation and incentive packages reinforce and reward the right sales behaviors in support of sales strategy
- designing and communicating effective incentive campaigns
- measuring the impact of incentive and compensation programs to ensure that objectives are met and problems are solved.

Most Important AOEs for Sales Enablement

In the validation phase of the study, participants in Sales Enablement roles were asked to rate the importance of AOEs to their success on the job using a 5-point scale (with 5 being critical; Table 4-5). Since a majority of survey respondents in the Sales Enablement role category were talent developers, their responses might have favored talent development AOEs (that is, sales talent development and sales coaching) over the other four AOEs. However, it is important to keep in mind that SMEs who participated in the interviews, focus groups, and content review phase of the study were representative of all enablement functions and, as a result, all six AOEs aligned to the sales enablement function are valid.

The following four AOEs were identified as the most important by sales talent developers:

- Sales Talent Development
- Sales Coaching
- Account Development and Retention
- Sales Tool and Process Improvement.

Table 4-5: Most Important AOEs for Sales Enablement

AOE	Areas of Expertise	Importance %
1	Sales Talent Development	85%
2	Sales Coaching	78%
3	Account Development and Retention	69%
4	Sales Tool and Process Improvement	65%
5	Sales Strategy Definition and Execution	62%
6	New Account Acquistion	60%
7	Complex Solution Definition and Positioning	55%
8	Sales Team Management	54%
9	Sales Talent Selection	52%
10	Partner Sales Support	48%
11	Sales Pipeline and Forecast Management	46%
12	Sales Incentive and Compensation Design	42%

Where Sales Enablement Professionals Spend Most Time

Participants in the Sales Enablement roles were also asked to select the top three AOEs where they spend the most time. The highest percentage of participants identified the following AOEs (Table 4-6):

- Sales Talent Development
- Sales Coaching
- Sales Tool and Process Improvement.

Table 4-6: Where Sales Enablement Personnel Spend Most Time

AOE	Area of Expertise	Time Spent %
1	Sales Talent Development	63%
2	Sales Coaching	53%
3	Sales Tool and Process Improvement	36%
4	Account Development and Retention	25%
5	Sales Talent Selection	18%
6	Complex Solution Definition and Positioning	16%
7	New Account Acquisition	16%
8	Sales Strategy Definition and Execution	16%
9	Sales Team Management	15%
10	Partner Sales Support	11%
11	Sales Pipeline and Forecast Management	7%
12	Sales Incentive and Compensation Design	5%

Conclusion

This chapter provided a more detailed description of AOEs and augmented this information with highlights from the validation survey results, in which participants responded to questions about the importance of the AOEs to their success on the job and the top three AOEs where they spend the most time. The most notable responses involved the relative importance of specific AOEs in comparison to the most time-consuming AOEs. For Sales Force roles, AOE 3 Complex Solution Definition and Positioning was both the most important and the most time-consuming. For Sales Management roles, AOE 2 Account Development and Retention was the most important, but AOE 1 New Account Acquisition was most time-consuming. For Sales Talent Development roles, AOE 10 Sales Talent Development, and AOE 8 Sales Coaching were both the most important and the most time-consuming AOEs.

5

FOUNDATIONAL COMPETENCIES

In addition to the areas of expertise (AOEs) that delineate the knowledge, skills, and expertise required for specific roles, the new ATD World-Class Sales Competency Model (WCSCM) contains 23 foundational competencies grouped into four clusters: collaboration, insight, solution, and effectiveness (Table 5-1). These foundational competencies are shared by all members of the sales profession.

Table 5-1: Foundational Competencies

Collaboration	Insight	Solution	Effectiveness
• Relationship Building • Alignment Building • Strategic Partnering • Teaming • Transformational Leadership • Customer Advocacy	• Business and Financial Acumen • Sector/Industry Insight • Evaluating Customer Experiences • Research Analysis	• Product/Service Acumen • Competitive Intelligence • Consultative Insight • Negotiating and Gaining Commitment • Complex Problem Solving	• Diversity Effectiveness • Global Awareness • Multigenerational Effectiveness • Sales Process Acumen • Technology Fluency • Project Management • Effective Communication • Ethical Decision Making

Descriptions of Foundational Competencies

The following is a brief description of the foundational competencies organized in the four clusters. For a detailed summary of key actions for these competencies, see Appendix B. For detailed results of the survey about the importance of individual actions for each competency, see Appendix D.

Collaboration Competencies

These competencies enable sales professionals to interact and work interdependently with others.

- **Relationship Building**—builds and nurtures positive internal and external relationships to facilitate customer satisfaction, personal effectiveness, and productive collaboration with others.
- **Alignment Building**—works effectively with others across organizational boundaries for the good of the organization.
- **Strategic Partnering**—actively seeks to understand, align with, and add value to the larger mission of the organization, including the go-to-market strategy.
- **Teaming**—works effectively in supporting or leading teams to ensure a clear focus, optimum cooperation, and high performance by all team members.
- **Transformational Leadership**—guides or supports customers through current challenges to optimize the current state and transition to a future desired state.
- **Customer Advocacy**—ensures that the concerns and priorities of the customer are understood and addressed, and that overall customer satisfaction is achieved.

Insight Competencies

These competencies enable sales professionals to develop a robust understanding of their customers and to use this insight to facilitate and guide customer decision making, through skills in information analysis and synthesis.

- **Business and Financial Acumen**—develops and uses sound business and financial understanding to develop meaningful business recommendations.
- **Sector/Industry Insight**—leverages understanding of emerging sector and industry developments as the basis for defining value-added solutions.
- **Evaluating Customer Experiences**—assesses the effectiveness and positive impact of solutions and communicates the results to stakeholders.
- **Research/Analysis**—proactively and systematically collects information needed for effective decision making, planning, relationship building, and well-targeted solutions.

Solution Competencies

These competencies enable sales professionals to develop strategies for identifying the right solution to customers' complex problems, generating enthusiasm for the solution they propose, competitively positioning the solution, and negotiating and gaining commitment.

- **Product/Service Acumen**—demonstrates a solid understanding of the company's products and services and their value proposition.
- **Competitive Intelligence**—applies competitive insight to effectively differentiate and position solutions.
- **Consultative Insight**—provides the informed experience, breadth of insight, and robust exploration essential for helping customers to make an optimum decision.
- **Negotiating and Gaining Commitment**—helps align all stakeholder interests to create a win/win balance that demonstrates mutual benefit, increases the probability of commitment, and drives the opportunity to closure.
- **Complex Problem Solving**—creatively brings new or alternative perspectives forward for consideration in order to overcome complex challenges.

Effectiveness Competencies

These competencies enable sales professionals to deal with accelerating change and the dynamic nature of the sales environment by demonstrating personal and professional effectiveness and responsibility.

- **Diversity Effectiveness**—values diversity (gender, ethnic, racial, cultural) and effectively leverages the insights and experiences of others to achieve goals and establish a stimulating, productive work environment.
- **Global Awareness**—understands the interconnectedness of modern business and works effectively within the global workplace.
- **Multigenerational Effectiveness**—understands intergenerational differences and approaches work-related interactions based on these differences to ensure optimum results.
- **Sales Process Acumen**—demonstrates a solid understanding of the company's selling process and aligns personal activities to the prescribed roles and responsibilities in the selling process.
- **Technology Fluency**—understands the contributions that technology makes to optimizing productivity and actively incorporates technology into work processes.
- **Project Management**—applies basic project management methods to ensure the successful progress of critical tasks.
- **Effective Communication and Presentation**—prepares clear, concise, and persuasive customer and internal communications, demonstrating effective writing and presentation skills and active listening, and projecting a credible image.
- **Ethical Decision Making**—adheres to ethical standards of personal conduct and business rules when making decisions or executing tasks.

Relative Importance of Foundational Competencies

In the validation phase of the study, participants were asked to rate the importance of foundational competencies to their success on the job using a 5-point scale (with 5 being critical).

The following three foundational competencies were identified as the most important by survey participants:

- Ethical Decision Making
- Relationship Building
- Customer Advocacy.

Average importance ratings for the top 10 foundational competencies are summarized in descending order (Table 5-2).

Table 5-2: Top 10 Foundational Competencies

Clusters	Foundational Competency	Averages
Effectiveness	Ethical Decision Making	4.63
Collaboration	Relationship Building	4.49
Collaboration	Customer Advocacy	4.40
Solution	Product/Service Acumen	4.38
Collaboration	Strategic Partnering	4.26
Effectiveness	Effective Communication and Presentation	4.26
Solution	Complex Problem Solving	4.21
Effectiveness	Diversity Effectiveness	4.21
Effectiveness	Project Management	4.20
Collaboration	Alignment Building	4.15

The average importance ratings for all foundational competencies are summarized, grouped by competency clusters (Collaboration, Insight, Solution, and Effectiveness) and appearing in descending order of importance within each cluster (Table 5-3).

Table 5-3: Foundational Competencies—Importance Ratings

Cluster 1: Collaboration	Averages
Relationship Building	4.49
Customer Advocacy	4.40
Strategic Partnering	4.26
Alignment Building	4.15
Transformational Leadership	4.15
Teaming	3.98
Cluster 2: Insight	**Averages**
Evaluating Customer Experiences	4.09
Research/Analysis	4.00
Business and Financial Acumen	3.97
Sector/Industry Insight	3.92
Cluster 3: Solution	**Averages**
Product/Service Acumen	4.38
Complex Problem Solving	4.21
Consultative Insight	3.92
Negotiating and Gaining Commitment	3.89
Competitive Intelligence	3.80
Cluster 4: Effectiveness	**Averages**
Diversity Effectiveness	4.21
Ethical Decision Making	4.63
Effective Communication and Presentation	4.26

Cluster 4: Effectiveness	Averages
Project Management	4.20
Sales Process Acumen	4.05
Technology Fluency	3.91
Multigenerational Effectiveness	3.79
Global Awareness	3.35

Conclusion

This chapter presented a more detailed description of the 23 foundational competencies shared by all members of the sales ecosystem and augmented this information with highlights from the validation survey results, in which participants were asked to rate the importance of these competencies to their success on the job. Respondents selected the following 10 competencies as most important:

- Relationship Building
- Ethical Decision Making
- Customer Advocacy
- Product Services Acumen
- Strategic Planning
- Effective Communication and Presentation
- Complex Problem Solving
- Diversity Effectiveness
- Project Management
- Alignment Building

6

HOW ORGANIZATIONS CAN USE THE NEW MODEL

The new ATD World-Class Sales Competency Model (WCSCM), like any other competency model, is a means to an end, not an end in and of itself. It provides sales organizations with a state-of-the-art competency framework that can be a critical tool to achieve a variety of sales talent management goals, such as:

- assessing sales competencies to identify competency gaps at individual, work group, and organizational levels, and to use the insights gained to guide the organization's investment in acquiring, developing, and retaining sales talent to fill the competency gaps and stay competitive
- conducting capability and capacity analysis to determine an organization's sales talent strengths and vulnerabilities and to prepare staffing and development plans for hiring and developing the needed sales talent in sufficient numbers to meet business needs
- preparing competency-based job descriptions to attract, hire, and develop sales talent in tight and competitive sales labor markets
- developing competency-based hiring guides for sales managers and sales recruiters to screen and hire sales talent with the right competencies to fill the sales competency gaps and help the organization remain competitive
- developing competency-based career lattices to enable career planning and development by individual sales professionals, helping them to develop business-essential sales competencies and enhance their careers within the organization
- defining and designing sales learning and talent development solutions to help sales professionals prepare individual development plans and acquire and maintain business-essential competencies in support of the organization's business objectives.

This chapter describes how sales organizations can use the new ATD WCSCM to achieve a variety of sales talent management goals in support of their business objectives.

Specific instructions are provided to help various groups and functions use the new ATD model to define, design, develop, deploy, and evaluate a wide range of sales talent management solutions (Figure 6-1).

Figure 6-1: Talent Management Solutions Enabled by WCSCM

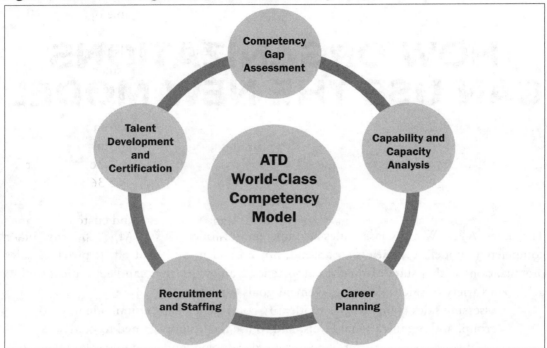

Competency Gap Assessment

The objective standard of excellence defined by the new WCSCM can serve as the basis for determining strengths and opportunities for development for all members of the sales ecosystem. The key knowledge, skills, and actions identified and validated for AOEs and foundational competencies provide a rich source of insight for building assessment tools to determine competency gaps at individual, work group, and organizational levels. The assessment results can then be used to determine appropriate investment in sales talent development and in hiring and staffing plans.

How to Conduct a Competency Gap Assessment

The following sections describe a four-phase process for building and implementing a competency assessment tool for your organization using the new ATD WCSCM.

Phase 1. Planning and Instrumentation

The objectives of this phase are to set up a successful assessment process, develop an assessment plan, identify assessment participants, and develop assessment and analysis procedures and tools. To accomplish these objectives, take the following steps:

1. Obtain needed business sponsorship and endorsement for completing the assessment.
2. Finalize the assessment requirements by answering questions such as:
   - How many sales roles will be assessed and how many individuals will be in each role?
   - Are you assessing everyone in a role or a representative sample of individuals in the role?
   - Is this a 90-degree assessment (asking only sales professionals to conduct self-assessment), 180-degree assessment (self- and manager assessment), 270-degree (self-, manager, and peer assessment), or a complete 360-degree assessment (including select customers in the assessment process)?
3. Identify a list of participants for the assessment and obtain their background information (for example, job title, location, business unit, and function).
4. Identify managers, peers, and select customers of participants and obtain their contact information, depending on whether it is a 180-, 270-, or 360-degree assessment.
5. Prepare messages to participants and their managers, peers, and customers (for example, invitation emails, frequently asked questions, and instructions on how to access and complete the assessment tools).
6. Define data collection and analysis procedures.
7. Build a customized assessment tool, leveraging the WCSCM. (See Appendix E.1: Job Aid for Building Customized Self-Assessment Tools.)
8. Send invitations and instructions to participants and their managers, peers, and/or customers to participate in the competency assessment.

Phase 2. Setting Proficiency Targets

The objective of this phase is to determine the criticality of AOEs and competencies to the success of the organization. This task will help determine the desired proficiency levels to be used as criteria for determining competency gaps. The information will also be used for sales capability and capacity planning. To accomplish these objectives, take the following steps:

1. Identify a small but representative group of organizational leaders (for example, between six and 12, depending on the size of organization) to set the proficiency targets. Candidates for this group include business sponsors and strategic influencers and subject matter experts (SMEs) in the organization.
2. Prepare a tool to be used by organizational leaders to set proficiency targets. (See Appendix E.2: Setting Proficiency Targets for Competency Assessment, for a template.) Note that the key skills and key knowledge for the new WCSCM for AOE 1 (New Account Acquisition) have been added to the template. Replace these items, if needed. Once all items from the customized assessment tool have been added, provide the organizational leaders.

3. Refer to the following instructions to set proficiency targets:

Using your knowledge of the organization's strategic business direction, as well as your own personal experiences, determine how critical each of the following items is to the success of the business, using a 5-point scale:

   5= Very Critical

   4 = Critical

   3 = Important

   2 = Somewhat Important

   1 = Less Important.

4. Collect proficiency targets from individual leaders, aggregate their input, set a single proficiency target for each item, and obtain approval from business sponsors. (See Appendix E.3: Aggregating and Finalizing Proficiency Targets, for a template.)

Phase 3. Performing a Competency Gap Assessment

The objective of this phase is to collect assessment data from participants (90-degree) and, if needed, from their managers (180-degree), their peers (270-degree), and select customers (360-degree). This phase comprises the following steps:

1. Monitor and encourage sales professionals to access and complete the "self-assessment" tool.
2. Monitor and encourage sales managers, peers, and select customers to complete their assessments of the sales professional being assessed.
3. Conduct appropriate follow-up communication to ensure full participation.
4. Extract and insert assessment data in the appropriate analysis tools. Data visualization tools can help you identify patterns and red flags, as well as transform assessment results into meaningful and digestible insights.

Phase 4. Competency Gap Analysis and Reporting

The objectives of this phase are to analyze the assessment data collected in Phase 2, to conduct individual and group competency gap analysis, and to prepare reports. This phase comprises the following steps:

1. Analyze the data collected and calculate the gap between self-rating and proficiency targets set by the organizational leaders. The size of the gap determines either competency strength or opportunities for competency development.
2. Create a chart that compares self-assessment results with assessments conducted by manager, peer, and/or customer (Figure 6-2).
3. Prepare individual reports. Each sales professional should receive his or her competency assessment results, which graphically and numerically show the gap between self-assessment; the proficiency targets; and assessment by the manager, peer, and/or customer. Also prepare and report the top three competency strengths and the three competencies that most need development. (See Appendix E.4 for an example of an individual competency gap assessment report.)

4. Prepare group reports. These reports should show competency gaps for various groups, such as business units, geographies, or functions. Use the same example used in Appendix E.4 to create group competency gap assessment reports for various groups.

Figure 6-2: Comparing Self-Assessment Results with Proficiency Targets

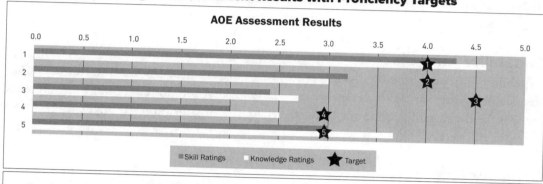

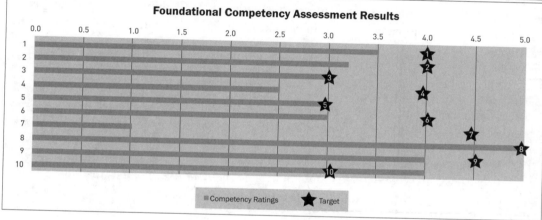

Competency gap assessments provide valuable insight to sales organization leaders, helping them to:

- Create staffing plans to fill sales competency gaps in business-critical areas with agility, through hiring and partnering.
- Allocate needed resources to create learning solutions that are targeted to thoroughly understand skill and knowledge needs of groups of sales professionals, rather than "nice-to-know" topics.
- Provide concrete insights to individuals engaged in competency development planning with their managers, enabling them to take advantage of existing resources to reduce their competency gaps.

Capability and Capacity Analysis

The new ATD WCSCM provides a set of state-of-the-art competencies (that is, capabilities) needed by sales professionals to help organizations achieve their business objectives.

The proficiency targets set during the competency assessment process determine how critical these capabilities are for the organization's success. The resulting competency gap assessment provides insight into sales competency strengths and gaps in the organization. Armed with these three data points—what is needed, how critical it is, and how close the organization is to having it—the organization can conduct capability and capacity analysis, using the results to prepare plans for acquiring and developing sales talent in the most critical capability areas where capacity is lowest.

Capability Analysis

Capability analysis provides insight into the most critical AOEs and foundational competencies for various roles in sales. These AOEs and foundational competencies are identified using the proficiency targets set by the organization's thought leaders and strategic influencers.

Capacity Analysis

Capacity analysis enables an organization to identify the number or proportion of sales professionals who have strength in critical AOEs and foundational competencies for their roles.

Case Example: Table 6-1 shows the most critical AOEs and foundational competencies for an account management role in a global sales organization. The checkmark in the column labeled Critical Capabilities indicates the AOEs and foundational competencies with a proficiency target of 4 or 5 on a 5-point scale, with 5 being very critical and 4 being critical. The table also shows the current capacity (that is, proportion of the account managers with strength in AOEs and foundational competencies). The columns headed Current Capacity show the proportion of account managers with a rating of 4 or 5 on the following 5-point Likert scale.

> 5 = Strength to Leverage
> 4 = Solid Strength
> 3 = Opportunity for Growth
> 2 = Development Need
> 1 = Strong Development Need.

Current capacity is reported at worldwide levels and for each of three geographies—Americas (AMS); Europe, Middle East, and Africa (EMEA); and Asia Pacific (APA). The example shows that for the critical AOEs of New Account Acquisition and Account Development and Retention, the entire organization has limited capacity (that is, fewer than half of sales professionals worldwide rated themselves at 4 or 5 on a 5-point scale). For New Account Acquisition, EMEA has the least capacity (38 percent), and AMS has the highest (56 percent). On the other hand, APA has the least capacity for Account Development and Retention. The greatest need in foundational competencies is for Sales Process Acumen in APA, but that is not a critical area. The greatest need in a critical area is in APA for Negotiating and Gaining Commitment.

Table 6-1: Example of Account Management Critical Capabilities and Current Capacity

Areas of Expertise (AOE) and Foundational Competencies	Critical Capabilities	Current Capacity			
		Worldwide	AMS	EMEA	APA
AOE					
New Account Acquisition	✓	49%	56%	38%	46%
AOE					
Account Development and Retention	✓	47%	50%	50%	42%
Complex Solution Definition and Positioning	✓	68%	69%	75%	62%
Partner Sales Support		68%	81%	50%	62%
Sales Pipeline and Forecast Management		59%	75%	63%	38%
Foundational Competencies					
Cluster 1: Collaboration					
Relationship Building	✓	76%	81%	88%	62%
Teaming		41%	50%	38%	31%
Cluster 2: Insight					
Business and Financial Acumen		70%	75%	88%	54%
Sector/Industry Insight	✓	57%	63%	63%	46%
Cluster 3: Solution					
Product Services Acumen		59%	56%	75%	54%
Negotiating and Gaining Commitment	✓	30%	31%	50%	15%
Competitive Intelligence	✓	36%	38%	50%	25%
Cluster 4: Effectiveness					
Ethical Decision Making	✓	59%	75%	63%	38%
Effective Communication and Presentation	✓	67%	63%	88%	58%
Sales Process Acumen		32%	50%	38%	8%

The insights gained from the analysis of critical capability and current capacity provide the leadership of a sales organization with the needed information to:

- Shape their hiring plans to recruit, screen, and select sales talent with the capabilities needed most.
- Establish partnership and talent exchanges with regions having higher capacity in the most critical capability areas.
- Allocate the needed resources to develop learning solutions for establishing critical AOEs and foundational competencies in the areas with lower capacity.

How to Conduct Capability and Capacity Analysis

The following sections describe a three-phase process for conducting a capability and capacity analysis, applying the new ATD WCSCM and using the competency gap assessment results described earlier.

Phase 1. Planning and Instrumentation

The objectives of this phase are to set up a successful capability and capacity analysis process, develop a plan for obtaining needed data, and develop analysis tools and reporting procedures and tools. To accomplish these objectives, take the following steps:

1. Obtain needed business sponsorship and endorsement for completing the analysis.
2. Identify the sales roles (for example, account managers, sales specialists, sales managers, sales coaches, sale trainers, and sales recruiters) that will be analyzed and determine the number of employees in each role in various business units, functions, and geographies.
3. Identify a list of participants in the analysis and obtain their background information (for example, job title, location, business unit, and function).
4. Define data collection and analysis procedures.

Phase 2. Obtaining Needed Data and Conducting Analysis

The objective of this phase is to collect needed data, conduct analysis, and report the results. To accomplish these objectives, take the following steps:

1. Obtain the results of proficiency targets set during Phase 2 of the Competency Gap Assessment process. If proficiency targets are not set, then follow the steps outlined in that phase and obtain input from organizational leaders and strategic influencers on the criticality of AOEs and foundational competencies to the success of the targeted roles.
2. Acquire the results of the Competency Gap Assessment during Phase 3 of the Competency Gap Assessment process. If these results do not exist, then follow the steps outlined in that phase and obtain data on competency strengths of individuals within the targeted role.
3. Use the template provided in Appendix E.5: Capturing and Reporting Capability and Capacity Analysis to:
   - Identify and record AOEs where the proficiency targets are set by organizational leaders and strategic influencers as 4 or 5 on a 5-point scale, with 5 being very critical and 4 being critical.
   - Calculate and record percentages of individuals in the targeted role who have a rating of 4 or 5 for the AOEs and foundational competencies using the following 5-point Likert scale:
     - 5 = Strength to Leverage
     - 4 = Solid Strength
     - 3 = Opportunity for Growth
     - 2 = Development Need
     - 1 = Strong Development Need.
   - Group AOEs and foundational competencies into three categories (high, medium, and low capacity) using the following criteria:
     - low capacity: 0 percent to 33 percent of individuals in the role have ratings of 4 or 5
     - medium capacity: 34 percent to 66 percent of individuals in the role have ratings of 4 or 5
     - high capacity: 67 percent to 100 percent of individuals in the role have ratings of 4 or 5.

4. Report on the criticality of AOEs and foundational competencies and their current capacity for all targeted roles in various regions, functions, and business units.

Phase 3. Leveraging Capability and Capacity Analysis Results

The objectives of this phase are to leverage the results to prepare or augment sales talent acquisition and development plans and to create necessary justification to obtain needed resources. To accomplish these objectives, take the following steps for all targeted roles:

1. Identify AOEs and foundational competencies that:
   ○ are *critical*; that is, their proficient targets are set as critical (4) or very critical (5)
   ○ have *low or medium capacity;* that is, less than 66 percent of professionals in the role have ratings of 4 (Solid Strength) or 5 (Strength to Leverage).
2. Determine the scope of need by repeating the first step wherever necessary to differentiate among various regions, functions, and business units.
3. Prepare or augment hiring plans to acquire sales talent (through hiring and/or contracting) for critical but low/medium capacity AOEs and foundational competencies.
4. Update learning and development plans to create learning and development solutions for critical AOEs and foundational competencies with low and medium capacity.
5. Prepare needed justification and business cases to obtain needed funding and resources to implement hiring and development plans to build needed critical capabilities in low-capacity areas in targeted roles.

Career Planning

The new WCSCM forms the basis for sales *role definitions* as well as requirements for *career movements,* allowing sales organizations to set objective employee expectations by creating career paths. These career paths can provide sales professionals with a range of options to progress in their careers within the sales ecosystem, including:

- lateral—moving across
- exploratory—investigating possibilities
- enrichment—growing in place
- realignment—stepping back
- vertical—moving up
- diagonal—moving up and across
- relocation—moving out.

These options will help sales professionals to continue to grow and develop throughout their careers, gathering many valuable experiences along the way. The career paths are intended to:

- Map various job titles (for example, inside sales representative, territory account manager, account executive) within a role (such as account management) along a continuum to demonstrate development and career growth in various directions, such as upward (vertical), diagonal, and horizontal (lateral).

- Illustrate interrelationships among various job titles and roles, demonstrating how various roles serve as feeders to each other and create career opportunities and mobility for members of the sales ecosystem.
- Provide descriptions and requirements for individual sales roles and their pivotal job titles, including:
  - **scope**—What will an individual in the role be doing?
  - **key responsibilities**—What will an individual in the role be held accountable for?
  - **competencies**—What competencies does an individual need to perform the role?

The following section describes how organizations can use the new WCSCM to create job descriptions and career paths.

Creating Job Descriptions

Organizations can use the new model to update their existing job descriptions and/or create new ones in the context of the organization's strategic direction. They can create a template for preparing a job description that illustrates the definition of a role; for example, Account Management, and individual job titles within the role (Inside Sales Representative, Territory Account Manager, and Account Executive) (Figure 6-3). The job description, then, would provide the following information about the role and job titles within the role:

- list of job titles (Inside Sales Representative, Territory Account Manager, Account Executive) within the role (Account Management)
- role description
- key responsibilities for individual jobs titles within the role
- shared responsibilities
- AOEs and foundational competencies.

Creating Career Paths

Organizations can leverage the new model to create or update existing career paths for upward movement within a role or for lateral movement among various roles within the sales ecosystem.

For example, an inside sales representative (ISR) in the account management role can advance within the role by becoming a territory account manager (TAM) and then an account executive (AE) or can make a lateral career move to a more technical role (such as sales specialist; Figure 6-4). The individual job descriptions identify the key knowledge, skills, and actions required for these roles and allow individuals to create a personalized career development plan.

Figure 6-3: Example: Job Description

Function: Sales Force Job Titles: Inside Sales Representative (ISR) Territory Account Manager (TAM) Account Executive (AE) Role Description: Serves . . .		Role: Account Manager	
KEY RESPONSIBILITIES			
Inside Sales Representative (ISR)	Territory Account Manager (TAM)		Account Executive (AE)
• . . . • . . .	• . . . • . . .		• . . . • . . .
Shared Responsibilities			
• . . .	• . . .		• . . .
Competencies			
Areas of Expertise			
Inside Sales Representative (ISR)	Territory Account Manager (TAM)		Account Executive (AE)
• . . . • . . .	• . . . • . . .		• . . . • . . .
Foundational Competencies			
• . . .	• . . .	• . . .	• . . .

Figure 6-4: Example: Sales Career Lattice

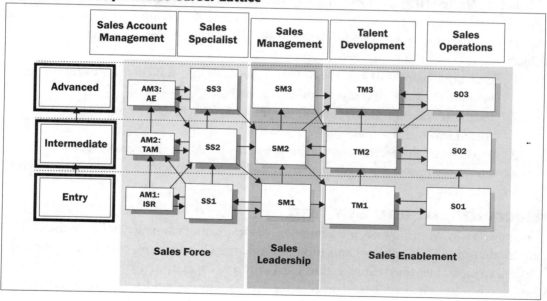

The following section describes a three-phase process for building career paths by leveraging the new ATD WCSCM.

Phase 1. Planning and Instrumentation

The objectives of this phase are to set up a successful process for building and validating career paths and job descriptions and to identify and engage stakeholders and SMEs. To fulfill these objectives, take the following steps:

1. Identify and collaborate with project stakeholders to finalize the list of roles and job titles within each role.
2. Obtain and review relevant documents and collateral (for example, company's existing sales job architecture, sales job descriptions, sales force planning documents).
3. Identify and engage stakeholders and SMEs to provide input for building and validating career paths.
4. Develop data collection and analysis tools and templates.
5. Obtain commitment and endorsement from organizational leaders for building, validating, and obtaining approval for new job descriptions and career paths.

Phase 2. Building Preliminary Job Descriptions and Career Lattices

The objectives of this phase are to obtain and analyze needed input and to develop preliminary career paths. To achieve the objectives, follow these steps:

1. Conduct document analysis.
2. Obtain input from SMEs, organizational leaders, and strategic influencers.
3. Analyze and integrate the information collected.
4. Develop a preliminary version for the career paths and job descriptions.

Phase 3. Validating and Finalizing Job Descriptions and Career Lattices

The objectives of this phase are to validate and finalize the preliminary career paths and to obtain approval from stakeholders for their implementation. To accomplish these objectives, take the following steps:

1. Enlist the support of knowledgeable individuals and stakeholders to review and validate the job descriptions and career paths.
2. Facilitate focus groups or obtain input and feedback, as well as suggestions for improvement.
3. Revise the job descriptions and career paths based on validation feedback.
4. Obtain approval for implementation and integration within appropriate systems.

Recruitment and Staffing

The new WCSCM provides a solid foundation for creating competency-based sales hiring guides that can help a sales organization implement its hiring plans, thereby achieving the desired capacity identified through the "capability and capacity analysis" process described earlier. This section describes a process for creating hiring guides to screen, select, and recommend job candidates based on critical AOEs and foundational competencies.

Creating Hiring Guides With the WCSCM

A hiring guide is a job aid that provides sales recruiters and hiring managers with situational and behavioral questions for assessing a job candidate's critical competencies during the selection process. Using AOEs and foundational competencies in the WCSCM to draft questions and to define selection criteria ensures accurate and objective assessment of target experiences. The hiring guide's rating system also provides a consistent framework for comparison of candidates. This framework is designed to support the selection of the most appropriate candidate for the sales role being filled.

An AOE can be leveraged to create a behavioral question for a sales hiring guide (Table 6-2). Note that the key skills, knowledge, and actions from the AOE are used to evaluate the candidate's responses.

Table 6-2: Example: Hiring Guide Situational Behavioral Based on an AOE

1. New Account Acquisition—Pursues opportunities and acquires new accounts by identifying and qualifying opportunities; systematically researching prospects; identifying and prioritizing prospect needs; aligning value propositions with needs and key performance indicators (KPIs) of prospects; proposing and competitively positioning solutions; and negotiating and closing.	RATING

Examples:	Question(s):
• Uses techniques for handling objections and drawbacks • Adjusts engagement tactics based on a careful reading of a prospect's receptiveness • Executes hunting and discovery efforts with persistence in the face of rejection • Tracks prospect business and financial health information, including KPIs • Generates and manages leads • [Insert additional examples as needed.]	**Tell me about a successful call—a time when you were able to break through a prospect's initial reluctance to make a sale.** [Look for evidence of the candidate's persistence and ability to "think on his/her feet" to handle objections without alienating customer, listen carefully, and adjust tactics based on an accurate reading of the customer's receptiveness.] **[ADVANCED ONLY:] Thorough research of prospective accounts is critical in any sales role. What tools and resources have you used to identify and prioritize potential customers?** [Look for use of conventional sources, social media, CRM prospect data, and industry and company press releases to identify and prioritize likely prospects based on their known business needs, KPIs, challenges, urgency of purchase, authority to buy, and other relevant factors.]

NOTES/COMMENTS:

Creating Hiring Guides in Five Steps

This section describes a five-step process for building customized sales hiring guides for your organization by leveraging the new ATD WCSCM. See Appendix F for a more detailed description of the process, as well as a template and examples for building a sales hiring guide to recruit, screen, and select sales candidates.

Step 1: Identify the Target Role and Define Business Requirements for It

A hiring guide can be created for a sales role in any of the three parts of the WCSCM (Sales Force, Sales Management and Leadership, and Sales Enablement). In this step, identify the role and, in collaboration with the hiring manager, identify the business requirements for the role.

Step 2: Identify and Select AOEs and Foundational Competencies

Referring to the results of the capability and capacity analysis and the appropriate part (for example, Sales Force) of the WCSCM, identify the most critical AOEs and foundational competencies that meet the hiring requirements identified in the first step of the process.

Step 3: Draft Situational Questions for AOEs and Foundational Competencies

For each AOE and foundational competency, identify a typical job situation in which an individual in the role would utilize this AOE or competency. The situation should include an open-ended question or request that provides an opportunity for the candidate to describe relevant experience(s) and actions that demonstrate his or her expertise.

Step 4: Identify Criteria for Evaluating the Candidate's Responses

Referring to the AOE and foundational competencies in the WCSCM, identify "Key action" and "Key knowledge or skill" that the candidate would need to handle the scenario(s) described in the "Question(s)" section. Place them in the "Examples" box next to the questions.

Step 5: Add Notes for the Interviewer After Each Scenario

In the "Look for . . ." part after each question, briefly describe the criteria by which candidate responses will be judged. What responses will indicate mastery of the foundational competency?

Sales Talent Development and Certification

Another critical component of the talent management solution set that organizations can create by leveraging the new WCSCM is sales talent development. The state-of-the-art AOEs and foundational competencies described in the new model, the results of competency gap assessment, especially at the group/organizational level, and the results of sales talent capacity analysis all provide rich sources of information for sales talent development professionals to define, design, develop, deploy, and evaluate learning and certification solutions for members of the sales ecosystem.

How to Build Learning Modules

The WCSCM can be adapted in three ways to build learning modules: select related foundational competencies that will benefit a majority of sales professionals; leverage AOEs specific to multiple sales roles (for example, Pipeline and Forecast Management or Sales Coaching) to build learning modules for those sales professionals; use key skills and knowledge areas in AOEs that are specific to individual roles that address the unique learning needs of those sales professionals (the latter also can be used as a basis for certification and accreditation programs).

These learning modules can be organized into learning road maps that sales professionals can use to organize their learning activities (Figure 6-5). The following example of a three-tier sales learning road map illustrates how learning modules are organized hierarchically to address sales talent development needs at three levels:

- role-specific AOE learning modules (Account Management, Technical Sales, Indirect Sales)
- shared AOE learning modules (Common Sales Force Learning Series)
- foundational competencies (Sales Foundation Learning Modules).

Figure 6-5: Example of a Sales Learning Road Map

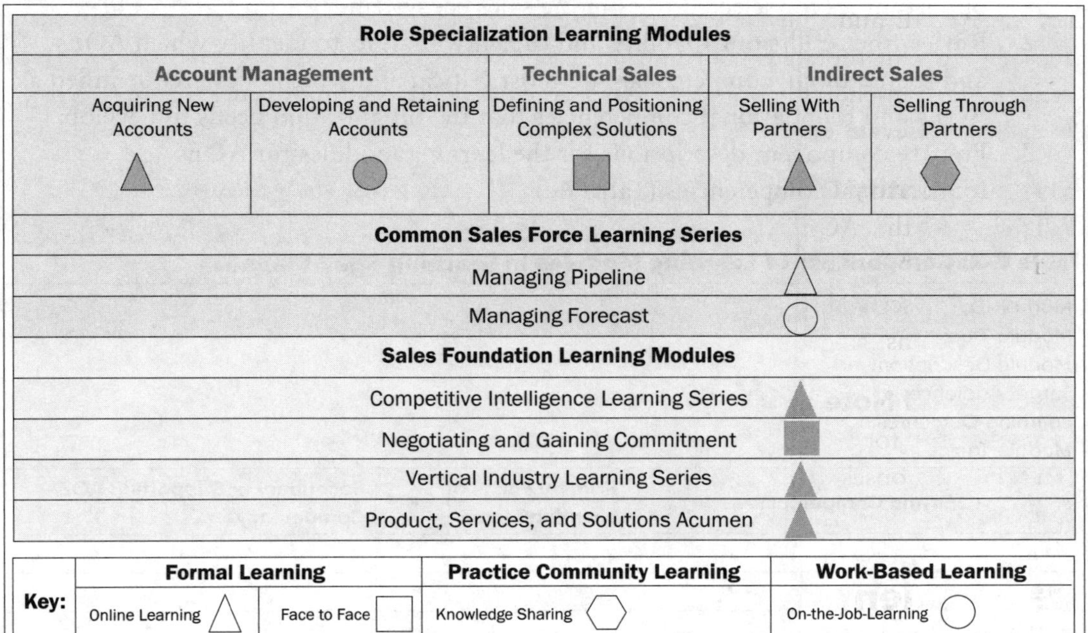

How to Build Learning Road Maps

The following section describes a three-phase process for building learning road maps by using the new ATD WCSCM.

Phase 1. Planning and Research

The objectives of this phase are to set up a successful process for building and validating learning road maps, identifying and engaging SMEs, and obtaining the results of competency gap assessment and capability and capacity assessment. To accomplish these objectives, take the following steps:

1. Identify and collaborate with project stakeholders to define the scope and coverage of learning road maps (that is, roles in the sales organization, AOEs, and foundational competencies for the roles selected).
2. Identify and inventory existing learning modules, including their descriptions, learning objectives, and a description of learning strategy and activities.
3. Obtain the results of competency gap assessments at the organizational level.
4. Obtain the results of capability and capacity analyses.
5. Identify and enlist the support of SMEs to provide input and to validate prototypes and provide timely feedback.

Phase 2. Building Preliminary Learning Road Maps

The objective of this phase is to leverage the new WCSCM and data collected in Phase 1 to develop preliminary learning road maps. To accomplish this objective, take the following steps:

1. Review the results of the organizational competency gaps assessment and identify the AOEs and foundational competencies with the highest development opportunities for selected roles in the sales ecosystem.
2. Review the results of capability and capacity analysis to identify which AOEs and foundational competencies are most critical and which ones are identified as AOEs and foundational competencies that the organization needs to develop.
3. Prepare component descriptions for the learning modules for AOEs and foundational competencies (Table 6-3).

Table 6-3: Components of Learning Modules in Learning Road Maps

Module ID:
Module Title:
Module Description:
Target Audience:
Learning Outcomes:
Module Topics

#	AOEs and Competencies	Primary Focus of Learning Module	Secondary or Supporting AOE/ Competency
1.1	. . .	✓	
1.2	. . .		

Delivery Options

Formal Learning		Practice Community Learning	Work-Based Learning
Self-directed	Instructor Led	On-the-Job Learning	Knowledge Sharing
✓			

Phase 3. Validating and Finalizing Job Descriptions and Career Maps

The objectives of this phase are to validate and finalize the preliminary learning road maps and paths and to obtain approval from stakeholders for their acquisition and development. To accomplish these objectives, follow these steps:

1. Enlist the support of SMEs to review and validate the learning road maps and descriptions of learning modules.
2. Facilitate focus groups or obtain feedback and suggestions for improvement.
3. Revise the learning module descriptions and learning road maps based on validation feedback.
4. Identify and mark existing learning modules that can be leveraged for building the new ones.
5. Obtain approval for acquisition, development, and deployment of learning road maps and their learning modules.

Conclusion

This chapter introduced some ideas to help organizations use the new WCSCM to create talent management solutions in support of their business objectives, as well as to consider additional ways that the new WCSCM could be leveraged. The next chapter presents ideas about how individuals in an organization can benefit from the new model.

7

HOW INDIVIDUALS CAN USE THE NEW MODEL

In addition to benefiting sales organizations, the new ATD sales competency model can also benefit sales and sales enablement professionals. This includes those professionals who are a part of a contingent workforce (as an independent contractor or consultant) or who belong to small sales organizations that do not have formal sales enablement and talent management programs. The new WCSCM provides these individual members of the sales profession with state-of-the-art standards and benchmarks to assess their current competency strengths and development opportunities. They can then use the insights gained to prepare a development plan to enhance their current job performance or to develop competencies for a desired future role in sales.

This chapter provides guidelines for how individual members of the sales profession can use the new ATD WCSCM to assess their sales competencies and then prepare an individual development plan to seek learning opportunities in an informed and structured manner, whether to enhance their current job performances or to advance their careers.

Competency Assessment

The role-specific areas of expertise (AOEs) and common foundational competencies in the new WCSCM define for individual members of the sales ecosystem the state-of-the-art competencies that they need to succeed in the dynamic sales profession. Reviewing the key knowledge areas, skills, and actions in the AOEs aligned to their current roles (for example, account management, sales management, and sales talent development) identifies what these individuals need to succeed in those roles. This study also provides information on relative importance of AOEs and foundational competencies as a benchmark to enable sales professionals to assess their strengths and development needs. Assessing oneself in roles aligned to one's desired future role provides additional insights into competency development needs to prepare for the next career move.

Example: An inside sales representative can assess herself in two AOEs (New Account Acquisition and Account Development and Retention) and use the results to enhance her performance in her current role as an account manager. She can also assess herself on the Sales Coaching AOE to determine her strengths and development needs for two potential career moves—from account management to sales management or sales talent development.

Guidelines for Conducting a Competency Assessment

The following section describes a four-step process for conducting a competency gap assessment to determine competency strengths and development needs for enhancing current job performance and advancing a sales career.

Step 1: Planning

The objective of this step is to set up a successful competency gap assessment using these activities:

1. Refer to the appropriate part of the new WCSCM and identify AOEs aligned to your:
   o **current role.** For example, if you are an account manager responsible for acquiring, retaining, and growing Fortune 500 clients, select the following four AOEs: 1)New Account Acquisition, 2) Account Development and Retention, 3) Complex Solution Definition and Positioning, and 4) Sales Pipeline and Forecast Management.
   o **desired roles that you are considering.** For example, if you want to make a career move to sales management, select the following four AOEs: 5) Sales Pipeline and Forecast Management, 6) Sales Strategy Definition and Execution, 7) Sales Team Management, and 8) Sales Coaching.
2. Locate the detailed descriptions of key knowledge areas, skills, and actions for these AOEs in Appendix A.

Step 2: Building a Self-Assessment Tool

The objective of this step is to build a self-assessment tool customized to your current sales role and your desired role(s) with the following activities:

1. Locate the Self-Assessment Template in Appendix G.1.
2. Go to Appendix D: Validation Survey Results, Part 2, locate your selected AOEs, and copy and paste the following information from the appropriate tables into the template:
   o list of key knowledge areas and skills for your selected AOEs
   o importance rating provided for these items by sales professionals who participated in the validation survey for building the WCSCM
   o average importance ratings for all key knowledge and skills.

The completed table, filled out according to AOE 1, New Account Acquisition, for example, would include the key knowledge areas shown in Table 7-1.

Table 7-1: Example of a Self-Assessment Tool for New Account Acquisition AOE

Current AOEs AOE: New Account Acquisition	Importance Rating	Self-Rating	Gap
Key Knowledge Items	**3.94**		
Product/service features, drawbacks, benefits, and value propositions	4.60		
Prospect business and financial health information, including key performance indicators (KPIs)	3.92		
Resource knowledge (e.g., marketing/industry, technical, pricing, legal, delivery, and fulfillment)	4.13		
Lead generation and management procedures	3.90		
Hunting and opportunity discovery techniques and best practices	4.13		
Objection and drawbacks handling techniques	4.06		
Competitive analysis and positioning resources	3.94		
Opportunity qualification and sizing techniques	3.92		
Sales cycle management techniques	3.55		
Social media sites and connectivity applications	2.88		
Company's selling process	3.65		
Company's core competencies	4.23		
Company's pricing guidelines, including discount and approval process	3.85		
Customer relationship management (CRM) best practices	3.67		
Buyers' business challenges and their drivers	4.50		
Business standards of conduct and ethical business practices	4.04		

Step 3: Performing an Assessment

The goal of this step is to assess yourself on your selected AOEs and all foundational competencies using the activities as follows:

1. Complete your selected AOE self-assessment by rating the knowledge and skill items using the following 5-point scale:

    5 = Strength to Leverage

    4 = Solid Strength

    3 = Opportunity for Growth

    2 = Development Need

    1 = Strong Development Need.

2. Calculate your average self-rating for all key knowledge areas and skills.
3. Locate the foundational competency self-assessment instrument in Appendix G.2.
4. Rate yourself on all foundational competencies using the following 5-point scale:

    5 = Strength to Leverage

    4 = Solid Strength

    3 = Opportunity for Growth

    2 = Development Need

    1 = Strong Development Need.

5. Calculate your average self-rating for each of the competencies.

Step 4: Completing a Gap Analysis

The objective of this step is identify your competency strengths and development opportunities with the following activities:

1. For both AOEs and foundational competencies, compare your self-rating and the importance rating, calculate the difference between both scores, and place it in the gap column.
2. Use the following guideline to determine your strengths and development opportunities:
   - Subtract your self-rating for each item from the Importance Rating to calculate the gap at individual knowledge and skill items and for the average of all items. A completed gap assessment for the first AOE, New Account Acquisition, lists these calculated ratings for key knowledge and skill areas (Table 7-2).
3. Identify your knowledge and skill strengths or development needs using the following guide:

Solid Strength = -2.1 or less
Strength = -1.1 to -2.0
Within Range = -1.0 to +1.0
Development Need = +1.1 to +2.0
Strong Development Need = +2.1 or above

Table 7-2: Example of a Gap Analysis Completed by an Account Manager

Current AOEs AOE: New Account Acquisition	Importance Rating	Self-Rating	Gap
Key Knowledge Areas	Average for all: 3.94	Average for all: 3.16	+ 0.78
Product/service features, drawbacks, benefits, and value propositions	4.60	3.0	+ 1.60
Prospect business and financial health information, including key performance indicators (KPIs)	3.92	4.0	- 0.08
Resource knowledge (e.g., marketing/industry, technical, pricing, legal, delivery, and fulfillment)	4.13	3.0	+ 1.13
Lead generation and management procedures	3.90	3.0	+ 0.90
Hunting and opportunity discovery techniques and best practices	4.13	2.0	+ 2.13
Objection and drawbacks handling techniques	4.06	3.5	+ 0.56
Competitive analysis and positioning resources	3.94	2.5	+ 1.44
Opportunity qualification and sizing techniques	3.92	4.0	- 0.08
Sales cycle management techniques	3.55	3.0	+ 0.55
Social media sites and connectivity applications	2.88	2.0	+ 0.88
Company's selling process	3.65	4.0	- 0.35
Company's core competencies	4.23	4.5	- 0.27
Company's pricing guidelines including discount and approval process	3.85	4.0	- 0.15

Current AOEs AOE: New Account Acquisition	Importance Rating	Self-Rating	Gap
Customer relationship management (CRM) best practices	3.67	1.5	+ 2.17
Buyers' business challenges and their drivers	4.50	2.5	+ 2.00
Business standards of conduct and ethical business practices	4.04	4.0	+ 0.04

Individual Development Planning

The new WCSCM and the results of competency gap assessments provide individual sales and sales enablement professionals with a rich source of information and insights needed to prepare an individual development plan. Such a plan can be used to enhance current job performance by focusing on the development of skills and knowledge critical to current work and advance a career by focusing on the development of skills and knowledge critical to desired roles in the sales ecosystem.

The development plan can include a range of learning and development options, including formal learning and experience-based learning, along with a timeline and needed resources. The following sections present a process and a tool set for building an individual development plan.

The process of preparing an individual development plan (IDP) to guide sales competency development efforts consists of the following three steps:

Step 1: Select AOEs

The objective of this step is to identify targeted AOEs for current and future desired roles by performing the following activities:

1. Review the appropriate parts of the new WCSCM (Sales Force, Sales Management and Leadership, and Sales Enablement) in chapter 4 to identify AOEs that are aligned to your current role and desired future role.
2. Prioritize your selected AOEs by leveraging the criticality or importance of the data provided by professionals in each role and reported in the tables in chapter 4 for each AOE. For example, in Table 4-1, for customer-facing sales professionals, over 78 percent of Sales Force participants rated the following four AOEs as 4 (important) or 5 (critical) on a 5-point scale:
    ◦ New Account Acquisition (78 percent)
    ◦ Account Development and Retention (78 percent)
    ◦ Complex Solution Definition and Positioning (80 percent)
    ◦ Sales Pipeline and Forecast Management (78 percent)
3. Select the AOEs that are critical for your current role and desired future role and capture them in the Individual Development Plan Template in Appendix G.3 (Table 7-3).

Table 7-3: Example Showing AOEs Critical for Current and Future Roles for an Account Manager

Name:			Date:	
Current Role:		Desired Role:		
Current Role AOEs and Knowledge and Skill to Be Developed:				

AOE Title	AOE Knowledge and Skill to Be Developed	Learning and Development Options	Timeframe
New Account Acquisition (AOE 1)			
Account Development and Retention (AOE 2)			

Desired Role AOEs and Knowledge and Skill to Be Developed:			
AOE Title	AOE Knowledge and Skill to Be Developed	Learning and Development Options	Timeframe
Sales Coaching (AOE 8)			

Step 2: Identify Development Opportunities

The objective of this step is to identify high-priority development gaps. Complete the following activities:

1. Review the results of the gap analysis that you conducted in Step 4 of the competency assessment described earlier. The goal is to identify:
   - Knowledge and skills in your targeted AOEs that you identified as a "development need" (that is, a gap of 1.1 to 2.0 points) or a "strong development need" (a gap of 2.1 or above)
   - foundational competencies that you identified as a "development need" or a "strong development need."

     [Note: If you have not conducted a competency gap assessment, follow Steps 1 through 4 in the Competency Assessment section of this chapter.]

2. Using the Individual Development Plan Template in Appendix G.3, capture the knowledge and skills with the highest development needs for each AOE. Also list foundational competencies with the highest development needs (Table 7-4).

Table 7-4: Example of Knowledge/Skill Gaps for AOEs Critical to Current Role

Name:		Date:	
Current Role:	**Desired Role**		
Current Role AOEs and Knowledge and Skill to Be Developed			
AOE Title	**AOE Knowledge and Skill to Be Developed**	**Learning and Development Options**	**Timeframe**
New Account Acquisition (AOE 1)	Customer relationship management (CRM) best practices		
	Hunting and opportunity discovery techniques and best practices		
	Buyers' business challenges and their drivers		
	Product/service features, drawbacks, benefits, and value propositions		
	Competitive analysis and positioning resources		
	Resource knowledge (e.g., marketing/industry, technical, pricing, legal, delivery, and fulfillment)		
Account Development and Retention (AOE 2)			

Desired Role AOEs and Knowledge and Skill to Be Developed			
AOE Title	**AOE Knowledge and Skill to Be Developed**	**Learning and Development Options**	**Timeframe**
Sales Coaching (AOE#8)			

Foundational Competencies to Be Developed		
Foundational Competency Title	**Learning and Development Options**	**Timeframe**

Step 3: Select Learning Options

The objective of this step is to identify appropriate learning and development options. Activities include the following:

1. Review and select a preliminary list of learning options provided by your organization and/or external sales training providers for each knowledge area or skill in the AOE and for select foundational competencies.
2. Identify the needed resources and define a timeline to complete the options.

3. Record these options in your IDP template.
4. Review the completed IDP with your coach and/or manager or a talent development adviser for feasibility and finalize the plan.

Conclusion

This chapter introduced methods for individual sales professionals to assess their competency strengths and development needs and build development plans to enhance job performance and advance their careers. The flexibility of the new WCSCM allows users to adapt it to their own needs. Chapter 8 presents additional suggestions for adapting the model to an organization's requirements.

8

ADAPTING THE WCSCM TO YOUR ORGANIZATION

During the research phase of creating the new ATD WCSCM, special care was taken to be inclusive by selecting diverse samples of contributors from the following categories:

- geographies (Asia/Pacific, Europe, Middle East/Africa, Central and Latin America, and North America)
- industries (consulting, education and training, financial services, healthcare, manufacturing, retail, and technology)
- generations (Millennial, Generation X, and Baby Boomer)
- market segments (enterprise, mid-market, and small business).

As a result, the new model is focused at a broader level in order to be applicable to sales professionals in various industries, generations, and market segments worldwide. It provides sales organizations with a strong foundation and a starting point to customize the AOEs to fit the context of their industry, market, and geography, as well as the strategic priorities of their business, by adding, removing, and/or modifying skills, knowledge, and behaviors in each AOE.

This chapter provides guidelines for adapting and customizing the model to the unique needs of an organization.

Note: The new WCSCM is trademark- and copyright-protected content, with all rights reserved; to customize or license the model, written permission must be obtained prior to making any changes. To obtain permission, contact the Association for Talent Development at 800.628.2783 (customercare@td.org) or publications@td.org.

Factors to Consider When Customizing the Model

A number of issues can drive customization efforts. Examples include but are not limited to the following factors.

Size and Scope of Role Differentiation in the Sales Organization

The new model adopted generic roles (account management, sales management, sales talent developer) in order to fit organizations of any size. If roles are differentiated with more specific responsibilities in a sales organization, then consider further differentiating the key actions, skills, and knowledge areas in AOEs aligned to these roles. For example, if the account management role in the organization is differentiated by the type of customer, then try augmenting the content of AOEs for various job titles in the account management role, such as inside sales representative, territory account manager, enterprise account manager, and account executive.

Industry/Sector

Customization efforts could be driven by the sector (for example, finance) and even subsectors (such as banking or financial markets) to which one belongs. To contextualize the AOEs, the key actions, knowledge areas, and skills could be augmented with specific examples and details about sector dynamics, concepts, KPIs, challenges, value chain, and so on.

Geographical Reach

The new WCSCM is built to be applicable to a global workforce. Depending on the makeup and talent management priorities of the sales organization, the key actions, knowledge areas, and skills could be customized to fit the specific needs of particular regions or cultural or local government regulatory considerations.

Market Segment Served

Another factor to consider for customization is the customers' market segment (for example, small and midsize versus enterprise and corporate customers). Key actions, knowledge areas, and skills could be customized to better fit the dominant market segments that the sales organization serves.

Solutions Set

The new WCSCM is product and service agnostic. It was designed to be applicable to all kinds of products, services, and solutions. To better serve the unique aspects of a company's products and services, the model could be customized with examples featuring the unique dynamics of selling a particular solutions set.

Time Horizon

Because the new WCSCM is based on comprehensive research in trends and evolving sales practices, it is well suited to use both today and in the near future. Depending on the business challenges of a sales organization, key actions, knowledge areas, and skills could be customized according to an organization's talent challenges today, in the near future, or both.

Process for Customizing the New Model

The process for customizing the model should follow the same process that was used to prepare the new WCSCM (see Appendix C). A three-phase version of the process is described as follows.

- Phase 1: Planning for Customizing the Model
- Phase 2: Preparing the Customized Draft
- Phase 3: Validating and Finalizing the Customized Model.

Phase 1: Planning for Customizing the Model

The goals of this phase are to set up a successful customization plan, to define customization factors, and to identify and onboard stakeholders and SMEs to help with customization. Include the following activities:

- Collaborate with sales organization sponsors and stakeholders to define and finalize the customization requirements by clearly identifying the customization variables.
- Define a customization plan and timeline that includes major activities with designated individuals responsible for the activities.
- Identify and recruit top performers and knowledgeable individuals in the organization, such as SMEs, who represent the areas to be customized (for example, industry, market segment, geography, or solution set) to help with customization.

Phase 2: Preparing the Customized Draft

The goal of this phase is to prepare a preliminary draft of the customized WCSCM, based on SME/stakeholder input. Incorporate the following activities:

- Schedule interviews and/or focus groups with SMEs to obtain input on select AOEs, based on defined customization variables.
- Analyze collected input and revise, delete, and/or add new behaviors, skills, and knowledge areas for AOEs.
- Create a complete draft of each AOE and, if needed, adjust the key behaviors in the foundational competencies section.

Phase 3: Validating and Finalizing the Customized Model

The goal of this phase is to validate, finalize, and obtain approval for the customized WCSCM. Include these activities:

- Share the preliminary draft of the revised model with SMEs to obtain feedback and iteratively revise the draft of the customized WCSCM. The reviews can be either one-on-one or through focus groups.
- Create a complete version of the revised model and share it with stakeholders and business sponsors for review and approval.
- Implement feedback from stakeholders and advisors and finalize the customized WCSCM.

Conclusion

This chapter provided a rationale and a process for customizing the WCSCM to reflect the unique needs of an organization and its sales professionals. When customizing the WCSCM, it is important to ensure that AOEs and foundational competencies include authentic examples from an individual's solution set, industry, and market segment, and that examples are recognizable and relevant to the targeted sales professionals. This approach will enhance the usability of the model. Time horizon is also an important consideration when customizing the WCSCM. During the planning phase of the customization process, collaborate with business sponsors and strategic influencers in the organization to identify the organization's strategic business needs over a time horizon of three to five years and explore the business implications for the sales talent. This time horizon is reasonable because it gives a customized WCSCM greater longevity.

APPENDIX A

AREAS OF EXPERTISE DICTIONARY

The new ATD World-Class Sales Competency Model (WCSCM) defines 12 areas of expertise (AOEs). These AOEs are grouped together and aligned to the three major role categories in the sales ecosystem:

1. Sales Force
2. Sales Management and Leadership
3. Sales Enablement

Table A-1: The 12 AOEs and Their Aligned Sales Roles

Area of Expertise	Aligned to These Roles		
	Sales Force	Sales Management	Sales Enablement
1. New Account Acquisition	✓		
2. Account Development and Retention	✓		
3. Complex Solution Definition and Positioning	✓		
4. Partner Sales Support	✓		
5. Sales Pipeline and Forecast Management	✓	✓	
6. Sales Strategy Definition and Execution		✓	
7. Sales Team Management		✓	
8. Sales Coaching		✓	✓
9. Sales Talent Selection			✓
10. Sales Talent Development			✓
11. Sales Tool and Process Improvement			✓
12. Sales Incentive and Compensation Design			✓

Each AOE consists of five components:

1. **AOE Title and Definition**—identifies the AOE
2. **Key Knowledge Areas**—various knowledge areas that are critical to successful performance on the job
3. **Key Skills**—critical skills needed to perform various tasks related to the AOE
4. **Key Actions**—observable behaviors and activities required for effective performance in the AOE
5. **Sample Outputs**—examples of tangible outcomes produced by sales professionals in the AOE.

The following are the 12 AOEs with the key knowledge and skills, key actions, and sample outputs for each.

AOE 1: New Account Acquisition

Pursues opportunities and acquires new accounts by identifying and qualifying opportunities, systematically researching prospects, identifying and prioritizing prospect needs, aligning value propositions with business and personal needs and key performance indicators (KPIs) of prospects, proposing and competitively positioning solutions, and negotiating and gaining customer commitment.

AOE 1: Key Knowledge and Skills

Successful performance requires *knowledge* of:

1. product/service features, drawbacks, benefits, and value propositions
2. prospect business and financial health information, including KPIs
3. resource knowledge (such as marketing/industry, technical, pricing, legal, delivery, and fulfillment)
4. lead generation and management procedures
5. hunting and opportunity discovery techniques and best practices
6. objection and drawbacks handling techniques
7. competitive analysis and positioning resources
8. opportunity qualification and sizing techniques
9. sales cycle management techniques
10. social media sites and connectivity applications
11. company's selling process (including sales process phases, phase definitions, and the requirements to advance an opportunity from one phase)
12. company's core competencies
13. company's pricing guidelines, including discount and approval process
14. customer relationship management (CRM) best practices
15. buyers' business challenges and their drivers
16. business standards of conduct and ethical business practices.

Successful performance requires the *ability* to:

1. Define engagement strategies based on assessment of a prospect and likelihood to buy.
2. Adjust engagement tactics based on a careful reading of a prospect's receptiveness.

3. Execute hunting and opportunity discovery efforts with persistence in the face of rejection.

4. Engage prospects in an exploratory conversation about their needs by focusing on listening, analyzing the information, summarizing their needs to confirm understanding, and avoiding a direct sales pitch.

5. Leverage market and industry insights accurately when positioning offers.

6. Manage leads and ensure follow-up/follow-through.

7. Map prospect management structure and decision-making authority.

8. Track and manage multiple sales opportunities and prospect engagements.

9. Identify the prospect's purchase drivers (e.g., their needs, priorities, problems to be solved, or opportunities to be realized).

10. Adapt and deliver sales presentations that speak to the prospect's most urgent needs.

11. Follow the sales process and utilize integrated customer relationship management (CRM) systems to manage and advance opportunities to closure and provide complete, accurate, and timely information.

12. Pursue global sales opportunities with sensitivity to cultural differences.

13. Present value propositions in compelling stories.

14. Identify issues that might require a need to modify the sales approach.

AOE 1: Key Actions

A successful performer:

1. **Establishes a social media presence as a credible source of information worth following**—Builds and maintains a presence on social media (for example, blogs, LinkedIn, Twitter, YouTube, Facebook, and Pinterest) to establish a thought leadership voice by developing and continuously refreshing content (for example, tips, trend identification, product bulletins, and industry or market insights); uses social platforms to conduct real-time research and gain insight on customers or the competition using portable devices and applications.

2. **Uses social media to create new customer networks**—Identifies key players and high-altitude individuals in new vertical industries or organizations, establishes contact, and provides valuable insights to entice them.

3. **Researches and targets prospects**—Uses tools and resources (for example, conventional sources, social media, CRM prospect data, and industry and company press releases) to identify and prioritize likely prospects based on their known business needs, KPIs, challenges, urgency of purchase, authority to buy, and other relevant factors.

4. **Initiates interest-building engagements**—Uses introductory sales calls to generate immediate interest and establishes personal credibility to build an extended relationship; provides the prospect with a compelling reason to share their needs, challenges, and opportunities; listens carefully to uncover specific needs and priorities and to adapt the focus of the sales engagement as needed.

5. **Qualifies prospects**—Assesses the prospect's purchase readiness, purchase authority, and business health to determine the feasibility of pursuing

opportunities; gains an understanding of and uncovers the prospect's compelling reasons for taking action; and determines scope and nature of risk as a necessary input to developing appropriate pricing, risk management, and negotiation strategies.

6. **Develops winning proposals**—Engages and collaborates with technical, legal, and financial resources to develop a compelling proposal aligned with customer needs and requirements; prepares the necessary business justification to ensure internal and customer buy-in.

7. **Negotiates deals and drives opportunities to close**—Engages and collaborates with experts (for example, technical, legal, and financial) to define and execute a customer negotiation strategy using proven tools and methods; educates stakeholders on deal parameters and bargaining positions as deals are driven to closure.

8. **Follows company's sales process**—Uses the sales process to qualify, advance, present, propose, and close sales opportunities.

9. **Pursues global sales opportunities**—Incorporates a global perspective in sales planning and pursuit efforts to accommodate multinational customer decision makers in multiple locations around the world by being sensitive to local considerations (for example, culture, law, rules, and regulations).

AOE 1: Sample Outputs

Deliverables include the following:

1. **Strategic pursuit plan**—A well-defined game plan for acquiring new accounts, which describes major activities, a timeline, and exit criteria for researching, identifying, engaging, assessing, qualifying, and persuading new prospects.

2. **Prioritized prospect list**—A frequently updated and rank-ordered list of prospects to ensure effective, efficient, and timely prospect engagement.

3. **Targeted prospect business profile**—A concise summary of each prospect's business needs, KPIs, challenges, urgency of purchase, financial and business health, authority to buy, and other relevant factors.

4. **Responses to requests for information (RFI)**—Responses that meet the requirements and address prospect's KPIs.

5. **Sales proposals**—Proposals that articulate value propositions, competitively position the solutions, and address customer KPIs.

6. **Business cases and reference materials**—Business cases and references that address prospect and its industry and sector challenges and opportunities.

7. **Call planning sheet**—A frequently updated game plan for driving the opportunity to closure, including names of who is on customer's short list.

8. **Negotiation strategy**—A game plan or strategy for negotiating desired outcomes, including alternative options that prospect has and a walk-out position.

9. **Competition profiles**—An up-to-date list of competitors under consideration,

their strengths and weaknesses, and alternative solutions that they provide to the prospect.

10. **Marketing program feedback on effectiveness**—Results of assessment of the effectiveness and return on investment made on marketing and promotion efforts.

11. **Strategic online presence plan**—A well-defined game plan for posting information and insight to entice and engage potential prospects (including what, how, and when).

AOE 2: Account Development and Retention

Nurtures, grows, and maintains existing accounts by monitoring, measuring, and ensuring customer satisfaction; leveraging existing contract for up-selling and cross-selling opportunities; actively troubleshooting and resolving issues; countering competitive threats; and expanding customer network and champions.

AOE 2: Key Knowledge and Skills

Successful performance requires *knowledge* of:

1. account farming procedures and best practices—cultivating opportunities within existing accounts (for example, check-ins, sponsoring marketing initiatives)
2. account history and contacts (prior investments, account relationships)
3. account planning tools, templates, and procedures
4. business metrics (for example, health ratios, return on investment, total cost of ownership)
5. rules of engagement, rewards, and commission structure regarding win-backs
6. competitive information resources
7. contract administration and renewal processes and resources
8. customer-oriented vertical industry information resources (for example, Dun & bradstreet, analyst reports)
9. back-office administrative/order-entry procedures
10. product/service features, benefits, and value propositions
11. supply chain knowledge (lead times, response rates, global fulfillment processes)
12. client's business life cycle (for example, start-up, growth, maintain phase)

Successful performance requires the *ability* to:

1. Acquire and manage leads and referrals.
2. Develop, manage, and modify long-term sales strategies.
3. Coordinate and align all account activities within the account plan.
4. Apply sales process and pipeline management practices, tools, metrics, and policies to prioritize and manage selling.
5. Calculate business metrics and translate product/service features into value propositions.
6. Effectively engage and partner with customer executives and key functions (for example, purchasing).
7. Collaborate with procurement to show promised savings or efficiencies.

8. Leverage marketing programs to advance sales.
9. Leverage contract administration and renewal into opportunities for up-selling and cross-selling.
10. Manage total customer satisfaction to optimize relationships.
11. Set accurate customer expectations for order fulfillment (for example, lead times, response rates, fulfillment processes).
12. Translate competitive knowledge into relevant competitive countering messages.
13. Leverage testimonials and references from other customers to retain and grow the account.
14. Collaborate with account teams in various countries in global accounts.

AOE 2: Key Actions

A successful performer:

1. **Develops and maintains strategic account plans**—Balances the pursuit of immediate opportunities with long-term, more strategic account planning; adapts strategic account plans as required to leverage to new developments or changing circumstances.
2. **Gathers and maintains account intelligence**—Establishes and extends networks within the customer's business to stay current with emerging requirements; maps the customer organization to identify decision makers and decision-making processes, as well as key purchase stakeholders; and scans relevant external publications or websites for account-related business information or developments.
3. **Actively targets and shapes customer business planning**—Leverages customer contacts to identify, shape, and respond to emerging opportunities and to influence requests for proposals (RFPs) prior to their issue.
4. **Maintains customer satisfaction and resolves customer complaints**—Acts as the accountable individual for resolving customer issues (for example, order or service fulfillment and product quality), advocates for the customer within the organization, and strives to ensure customer satisfaction.
5. **Builds, nurtures, and extends client business relationships**—Widens the breadth and depth of account presence and frames sales messages in terms of the client's business needs rather than product features and benefits.
6. **Cultivates and achieves trusted advisor status**—Develops and maintains under-standing of the customer's business needs and challenges and market/industry context to ensure that value propositions are aligned and resonate with customer business needs; provides on-demand consultative advice and maintains credibility and trust.
7. **Protects and expands accounts**—Ensures that all contractual obligations are met and that customer satisfaction is achieved; monitors competitive activities in accounts and appropriately counters competitive messages while blocking future competitor inroads.

8. **Uses CRM as a tool to maintain account information**—Updates account information in CRM to ensure availability of accurate up-to-date information for pursuit of growth opportunities and for reporting to stakeholders

9. **Collaborates with multinational sales and customer teams**—Establishes and nurtures relationships with colleagues and customers of global accounts in various geographies with sensitivity to cultural differences and local laws and regulations.

AOE 2: Sample Outputs

Deliverables include the following:

1. **Strategic account plan**—A well-defined game plan for retaining and growing existing accounts, which describes customer needs, requirements, KPIs, major activities, timeline, and exit criteria for enhancing customer satisfaction and gaining higher share of customer wallet.

2. **Account profiles and customer organization maps**—A concise summary of a customer's business needs, KPIs, challenges, urgency of purchase, financial and business health, authority to buy, and other relevant information.

3. **Account-oriented documentation**—Examples include letters of intent, service-level agreements, contracts, and competitor analyses.

4. **Lead management strategies**—A clearly defined plan for identifying, tracking, utilizing, and managing leads and referrals.

5. **Service-level agreements**—Description of contracted services, including acceptance criteria and metrics for measuring success.

6. **Competitive analyses and position papers**—A clear picture of competitive presence in the account, including their share of wallet, their plans, and their status in the account.

7. **Solution road map and account transition plan**—A clear picture of company's evolving solution set and a description of key activities to help customer transition from current to future solutions.

8. **Up-to-date account information**—Customer information in the CRM reflecting an accurate picture of the account's information in areas that are critical to maintaining the account and growing the account's business.

AOE 3: Complex Solution Definition and Positioning

Drives or supports complex sales opportunities by translating business requirements into technical solution requirements; coordinating technical expertise; sizing, scoping, and defining delivery and deployment approach and timeline; identifying required resources; coordinating demonstrations and proof-of-concept; and supporting internal deal acceptance.

AOE 3: Key Knowledge and Skills

Successful performance requires *knowledge* of:

1. complex opportunity qualification techniques
2. product/service/solution technology (for example, concepts, uses)
3. business context and business impact of complex solutions
4. requirements analysis and management techniques
5. solution design methodologies, best practices, and trends
6. solution configuration frameworks or templates
7. solution design procedures and communication conventions (written/visual)
8. solution sizing criteria
9. technical trust-building and selling
10. sales process phases and at what phase in the process a solution is defined and positioned.

Successful performance requires the *ability* to:

1. Define detailed solution requirements.
2. Translate solution designs into meaningful customer benefits and align them to stakeholder needs.
3. Competitively position product or service and articulate its value in tangible or measurable terms.
4. Develop trusted advisor status with customers, by demonstrating solution acumen.
5. Communicate technical solutions to nontechnical audiences.
6. Ensure cost-effective solution deployment and delivery practices.
7. Manage technical teams and integrate their contributions.
8. Adhere to sales process phases to ensure that the steps leading up to defining and positioning a solution have been completed.

AOE 3: Key Actions

A successful performer:

1. **Performs technical qualifications**—Translates the customer's business or operational requirements into technical requirements; assesses the technical feasibility of a successful solution deployment; and builds technical credibility with clients to counter competitive arguments and advance the sale with the technical decision maker(s).
2. **Designs complex solutions**—Defines a solution architecture by identifying key solution components and describing their interrelationships; identifies the risks involved in making trade-offs; and validates solution ideas with customers, peers, and account teams to ensure solution integrity and feasibility.
3. **Customizes standard products or services**—Enlists and collaborates with subject matter experts (SMEs) to design custom solutions that accommodate a customer's requirements and/or protect current investments.
4. **Conducts technical demonstrations and benchmarks**—Demonstrates the features, benefits, business value, and competitive advantage of a solution; generates

proof-of-concept data; and leverages benchmark data to create a compelling business case for selecting the proposed solution.

5. **Sizes complex solutions**—Collaborates with functional experts (for example, colleagues in deployment, service delivery, finance, and legal) to accurately size a proposed solution; adapts solutions in response to new customer requirements, funding restrictions, the desire for a phased approach, or other factors.

6. **Articulates solution designs**—Positions complex solutions in a way that is understandable to technical stakeholders within the customer's environment; reviews all communications and proposals for accurate solution definition and identification of benefits.

7. **Defines deployment options**—Defines alternative deployment options (for example, rapid prototyping and staged deployment) and timeline associated with each option.

AOE 3: Sample Outputs

Deliverables include the following:

1. **Solution requirements document**—A precise description of business needs and requirements translated into solution requirements.

2. **Solution design specification**—A detailed blueprint for creating a complex solution.

3. **Prototypes and proof of concept**—Preliminary working drafts of solution components that demonstrate key solution features and are mapped to business requirements.

4. **Technical components of proposals**—Accurate and clear description of the solution and its components.

5. **Solution presentations**—Presentation and demonstration materials for communication with technical and nontechnical stakeholders.

6. **Business cases and reference materials**—Business cases and references that address how the solution meets customer business needs.

7. **Work flow/work breakdown structures**—A road map that provides the account team and customer with guidelines for development and deployment of the complex solution.

AOE 4: Partner Sales Support

Manages and supports indirect (channel) selling by preparing joint business and marketing plans; co-selling with partners; onboarding and training partners on company's strategies and priorities, products/solutions, and partner incentive programs; and advocating for partners internally and protecting their interests.

AOE 4: Key Knowledge and Skills

Successful performance requires *knowledge* of:

1. company indirect sales motion, strategy, and direction
2. rules of engagement with partners

3. partner business model and financial health
4. partner incentive programs
5. procedures for escalating and resolving partner issues
6. partner loyalty and commitment-building techniques
7. partner sales crediting processes and tools
8. partner types and functions (distributors, resellers, specialized partners)
9. sell-with, sell-through, sell-for techniques
10. partner skill requirements and certification processes
11. partner's selling process.

Successful performance requires the *ability* to:

1. Prepare joint business plans.
2. Enhance partner commitment and gain share of partner wallet.
3. Set service level agreement expectations with partners.
4. Expedite partner reporting and communications using automated tools (for example, CRM).
5. Ensure partner compliance to product or service certification requirements.
6. Ensure timely and accurate product/service updates to partners.
7. Implement partner performance assessments.
8. Influence operations to ensure timely and accurate payout to partners.
9. Leverage marketing programs and initiatives to advance partner selling.

AOE 4: Key Actions

A successful performer:

1. **Drives joint sales planning and forecasting**—Sets joint sales goals and metrics, defines a joint sales plan for achieving sales goals, and monitors partner activities for compliance to plan and, where warranted, make mid-course corrections to plan.
2. **Assesses and ensures partner's sales force readiness**—Assesses the talent of partner sales force to leverage strengths, identify weaknesses, and address gaps in leveraging partner training and certification programs.
3. **Motivates and educates partners**—Leverages marketing promotions and partner incentive programs to advance partner selling and enhance partner preference for products/services over the competition; ensures partners are adequately prepared for accurately positioning products/services by communicating training and certification requirements and facilitating partner enrollment in appropriate training programs.
4. **Cultivates partner business relationships**—Builds understanding of partner's business objectives, extends partner planning activities to the highest levels of the partner's organization, and clearly articulates the business advantages of partnering to expand the range of selling.
5. **Facilitates inventory balancing/clearance**—Monitors distributor warehouse turnover for optimum sell-through and collaborates with distributors in developing strategies and making the marketing investments needed to advance or accelerate end-point selling.

6. **Tracks investments in partner selling to determine business impact**—Uses partner self-reports or independent data to assess ROI for funds invested in partner.
7. **Troubleshoots partner sales crediting**—Actively works with operations team members to correct inaccuracies as well as to ensure timely crediting of partner sales.
8. **Collaborates in team selling and positioning**—Assists partner at critical sales cycle junctures (for example, positioning, negotiation, and closing) to sell with agility and, when appropriate, works internally to acquire optimum pricing or exemptions.

AOE 4: Sample Outputs

Deliverables include the following:

1. **Partner joint business plan**—A well-defined game plan for selling with and selling through partners, which describes joint goals, metrics, businesses requirements, major activities, timeline, and exit criteria for achieving profitable growth for both the partner and the company.
2. **Partner profile**—A concise summary of partner business needs, KPIs, challenges, strengths, potential contribution to the success of the company, and other relevant information.
3. **Partner performance assessment report**—Quarterly report on partner performance, including achievement of milestones and metrics and recommendations of mid-course correction.
4. **Inventory management and turnover metrics**—A set of metrics to assess joint selling, promotion efforts to clear inventory and move products, and solutions from company to partner and in turn to customers.
5. **Market investment funding plans**—Clearly defined plans for marketing investment made on behalf of the partner, along with metrics to measure results.
6. **Transformation plans**—Plans to enhance partners' loyalty and commitment and transform them from transactional to strategic partners.

AOE 5: Sales Pipeline and Forecast Management

Leverages the power of sales analytics to exploit sales opportunities and ensure achievement of business results by populating and managing the sales pipeline, managing and protecting margin, developing and monitoring sales forecasts, and using CRM systems.

AOE 5: Key Knowledge and Skills

Successful performance requires *knowledge* of:

1. sales process stages and requirements to advance from one stage to the next
2. big data-enabled analytics to manage the pipeline more effectively
3. CRM systems and tools
4. forecast discipline and associated methods/processes
5. forecast report templates and requirements

6. margin management requirements and techniques
7. sales analytics methods
8. company's pricing guidelines, including discount and approval process
9. financial basics (for example, balance sheet, income statement, and cash flow statement).

Successful performance requires the *ability* to:

1. Apply relevant account planning tools, templates, and procedures.
2. Manage and assess the quality, size, shape, and velocity of the sales pipeline.
3. Prepare accurate and timely sales forecasts.
4. Use margin requirements when qualifying opportunities and prospects to ensure profitability.
5. Build a sales pipeline of high-quality opportunities and disqualify unlikely and poorly fit opportunities.
6. Use CRM systems to enter relevant information for forecasting, resource allocation, and decision making.
7. Conduct win-loss analysis and share insights with other stakeholders.

AOE 5: Key Actions

A successful performer:

1. **Harnesses CRM to achieve sales objectives**—Utilizes CRM innovations and capabilities to automate, integrate, and expedite a range of sales tasks (for example, track and measure promotion campaigns, assess customer spend and churn, determine and set priorities around customer KPIs, synchronize schedules and appointments, communicate with customers, improve customer experiences, and coordinate planning and pursuit activities with partners).
2. **Develops and manages accurate sales pipelines**—Builds, monitors, and orchestrates sales pipelines to ensure business predictability, the identification of margin-rich opportunities, and the best investment of time and effort; applies CRM tools as central repository and an enabler to record, track, analyze, and report sales pipeline data; uses pipeline insights to prioritize pursuit activities and identify deals with the highest close potential; monitors pipeline activity to ensure active nurturing of all deals and constant movement of opportunities to close; and removes stalled deals out of the pipeline to improve forecast accuracy.
3. **Develops accurate sales forecasts and reports**—Develops, monitors, and communicates sales forecasts; leverages CRM capabilities to ensure accurate forecast predictability based on objective statistics; adjusts forecasts as required to accommodate emerging challenges or breakthroughs; and develops ad hoc and quarterly reports for management as required to facilitate business planning.
4. **Sets competitive pricing and protects margin**—Follows company's pricing guidelines to set competitive pricing and focuses customers on product value propositions and the financial returns associated with solutions; uses cross-selling and up-selling strategies to enhance profitability and to protect gross margin; applies pricing tools and pricing parameters appropriately in negotiating and

finalizing prices with customers; and executes margin management strategies at both the account and opportunity levels to ensure bottom-line profitability (for example, discounts, product mix, use of third-party or legacy products, and add-ons).

AOE 5: Sample Outputs

Deliverables include the following:

1. **Accurate and up-to-date pipeline report**—Including information such as size, shape, and velocity of pipelines.
2. **Accurate forecasts**—Including both regular and ad hoc forecast reports.
3. **Margin protection and recovery plan**—A game plan or strategy to protect margin and ensure profitability across the portfolio by focusing on margin-rich opportunities and utilizing up-sell and cross-sell techniques.
4. **Sales analytic reports (trends and predictions)**—Regular and ad hoc reports to alert account team members, business sponsors, and other stakeholders on actions to be taken.

AOE 6: Sales Strategy Definition and Execution

Develops and implements sales strategies appropriate to market segments and customer-unique needs by monitoring emerging market trends setting; the priorities, direction, and framework for more tactical sales planning; ensuring internal organizational buy-in; leveraging innovative sales practices and automated sales tools; translating the sales strategy to actionable plans and courses of action; empowering the team to execute the strategy; and setting metrics to measure success.

AOE 6: Key Knowledge and Skills

Successful performance requires *knowledge* of:

1. business profit/loss management methods
2. company business plans, market position, and strategic direction and goals
3. relationship between marketing efforts and initiatives and sales enablement
4. competitive knowledge and best practices
5. social media strategies and best practices
6. business standards of conduct and ethical business practices
7. cultural and market segment demographic shifts and diversity
8. ways to optimize online presence strategies, including social media for sales force and sales organization
9. executive relationship-building strategies
10. market dynamics (general and product/service-specific trends)
11. risk management and mitigation strategies
12. sales best practice and industry sales benchmarking resources
13. sales metrics, KPIs, and measurement methods
14. sales system/tool/process automation requirements.

Successful performance requires the *ability* to:

1. Respond to market challenges and opportunities systemically by developing actionable sales strategies.
2. Define sales force requirements based on analysis of industry/market dynamics.
3. Serve as a bridge between marketing and sales enablement by identifying sales activities that support marketing efforts and initiatives.
4. Share customer feedback about products and services with the company.
5. Span boundaries to develop cross-product/service line strategies.
6. Build executive sponsorship at the highest levels of the company.
7. Identify areas of risk and develop appropriate contingency plans.
8. Identify and leverage best sales practices within the organization.
9. Manage complex change or transformation programs for executing the sales strategy.
10. Optimize online presence strategies, including social media for sales force and sales organization.

AOE 6: Key Actions

A successful performer:

1. **Assesses the effectiveness of the current sales strategy**—Uses broad market/industry sources, expert opinion, and historical sales data to identify emerging threats, downward trends, and market expansion opportunities; assesses quarterly results, CRM data, and voice-from-the field feedback as the basis for assessing the effectiveness of current sales strategies in achieving business objectives; and conducts root-cause analyses to determine the scope and extent of change needed.
2. **Identifies and promotes effective and innovative sales practices**—Identifies key obstacles to sales effectiveness; adapts and implements competitive practices for sales improvement; and ensures sales teams have an understanding of the concept of sales effectiveness and follow adopted sales methodologies and sales processes.
3. **Creates strategic sales plans**—Develops and builds consensus for the strategic plans that set or revise the sales goals, direction, and priorities of the organization; works with SMEs to develop the tools and systems support envisioned; and monitors implementation to assess success and adjusts strategy as needed.
4. **Provides leadership to accelerate strategy implementation**—Develops communication and readiness strategies to generate enthusiasm for the strategy, motivate the effort needed for success, and provide the guidance essential for tactical sales planning; leverages technology; and uses events to personally champion strategy.
5. **Engages and aligns key players**—Seamlessly engages internal partners in marketing, HR, sales enablement, and compensation in the work of creating strategic sales plans.
6. **Defines and implements detailed plans to execute the strategy**—Defines actionable plans and courses of action along with metrics to implement the sales strategy; works with and empowers sales team to execute the strategy.

7. **Measures the impact of the sales strategy**—Assesses the effectiveness and business impact of the new sales strategy to take mid-course corrections in order to optimize the strategy and enhance its business impact using KPIs.

AOE 6: Sample Outputs

Deliverables include the following:

1. **Strategic sales plan**—A well-defined sales strategy appropriate to market segments, geographies, industries, and customer-unique needs, which enables sales teams to achieve their goals and metrics and contribute to profitable growth of the company.
2. **Change management strategies and presentations for implementing the strategy**—A well-articulated game plan or strategy for communicating and implementing needed changes for implementing the sales strategy systematically and with agility.
3. **Business requirements**—A well-defined set of needs for the sales strategy based on business objectives (for example, market share, revenue, and margin targets), along with company and customer KPIs, to guide sales strategy, definition, and implementation.
4. **Best practice repositories**—A set of evolving best practices in professional selling to inform strategy definition and implementation.
5. **Executive summaries, briefings, and dashboards**—A means for sharing sales strategy and implementation plans with business sponsors, sales teams, and other stakeholders.
6. **Knowledge-sharing documents**—Information containing lessons learned from deployment of the strategy.
7. **Partner-planning communication documents**—Information for sharing sales strategy with partners and ensure their buy-in.
8. **Detailed action plans**—Detailed courses of action for implementing sales strategy.
9. **Back-up plans**—Realistic mid-course correction plans to ensure successful implementation of sales strategy.
10. **Metrics to measure success**—Well-defined set of concrete in-process metrics (for example, number and size of opportunities in the pipeline) and terminal metrics (for example, win rate, revenue, and margin) to measure success of sales strategy.

AOE 7: Sales Team Management

Manages sales teams effectively by analyzing sales team data (for example, forecasts and progress to goals); ensuring achievement of metrics (for example, quota and margin attainment); allocating resources and managing budgets; attracting, selecting, onboarding, developing, coaching, motivating, promoting, and terminating personnel; conducting performance reviews and career planning; removing demotivating factors in the environment; and enhancing collective team competencies.

AOE 7: Key Knowledge and Skills

Successful performance requires *knowledge* of:

1. business standards of conduct and ethical guidelines
2. company key performance indicators (KPIs)
3. sales targets
4. sales incentive and compensation plans
5. CRM applications and their use
6. pipeline management methods/tools
7. performance management techniques
8. human resources policies and procedures
9. organizational and operational processes
10. management processes and tools
11. margin management techniques
12. supply chain/order fulfillment processes/procedures
13. sharePoint and repositories of sales collateral, tools, templates, etc.
14. available resources and approaches for sales talent development at individual and group level
15. sales force motivating and demotivating factors.

Successful performance requires the *ability* to:

1. Apply approved methods to personnel management (hiring, terminating, promoting).
2. Apply best practices in motivating employees and enhancing their morale and performance.
3. Assess individual or team strengths and weaknesses.
4. Build strategies for counteracting competitive tactics.
5. Ensure compliance to company policies and applicable local, national, and international laws and regulations.
6. Ensure sales force compliance to standards of conduct and ethical guidelines.
7. Identify and address sales force gaps (for example, training and hiring).
8. Build a succession or short-term replacement plan to deal with staff turnover and workload redistribution.
9. Manage business forecasts to ensure accuracy.
10. Manage operations to minimize costs or maximize profits.
11. Lead global, multicultural sales team.
12. Engage sales teams.
13. Maintain a talent pipeline.

AOE 7: Key Actions

A successful performer:

1. **Aligns tactical sales activities to strategic sales plans**—Aligns everyday sales activities to strategic goals of the organization and sets priorities and expectations; identifies and addresses organizational challenges or opportunities to implement strategic sales plans.

2. **Sets budget and controls costs that impact sales margins**—Establishes operating budgets, tracks spending, and drives cost-control and operational efficiencies; manages sales-related allowances and discounts to ensure appropriate margin; and re-allocates funding to address cost overruns.

3. **Aligns resources with opportunities**—Collaborates with local or regional colleagues to ensure optimum opportunity coverage using available resources; ensures optimum targeting of resources to the most appropriate opportunities.

4. **Ensures accurate forecasting**—Ensures use of innovative CRM-based planning and reporting tools/systems to establish consistency, promote accuracy, support optimum selling practices, and advance real-time management assessment; tracks performance against established metrics (for example, pipeline movement, account plans, and customer satisfaction); and develops and rolls up aggregate forecasts or financial reports.

5. **Hires, promotes, and terminates sales team members**—Reviews and selects qualified candidates, conducts interviews, facilitates new hire orientation, and sets expectations; identifies and promotes sales talent; provides counseling to address and resolve individual performance challenges; creates required documentation; and conducts terminations professionally and in compliance with company policy.

6. **Aligns reward and recognition strategies to performance goals**—Uses the most appropriate rewards to recognize excellence and advance overall sales performance; administers recognition and reward programs fairly to maintain morale and create high performance sales teams.

7. **Manages variety of sales management activities in a balanced way**—Manages time effectively and prioritizes key sales management activities (for example, hiring, coaching, forecasting, reporting, and planning).

8. **Leads a global, multicultural sales force**—Incorporates a global perspective in leading multi-national sales teams located in different time zones with cultural differences and varied local practices and regulations.

AOE 7: Sample Outputs

Deliverables include the following:

1. **Sales forecasts (synthesized/rolled-up)**—Accurate and timely forecast to be shared with business executives and other stakeholders for timely decision making.

2. **Sales force incentive plan**—Fair and equitable plan to motivate the sales team members and drive and reward the right performance.

3. **Employee performance review**—Accurate and objective performance data, along with well-documented decisions and plans of action.

4. **Employee termination documents**—Corporate template documents used to provide required information regarding employee termination in compliance with company policy.

5. **Budgets and expenditure control plans**—Documents that ensure appropriate investment and management of cost of sales.
6. **Hiring interview instruments and methods**—Situational questions and objective process to accurately assess candidates on business-essential competencies and fit for the job.
7. **New hire training plan**—A well-defined onboarding plan to ensure speedy integration and improvement of time to productivity.
8. **Development plans**—Individual and team training and development plans.
9. **Sales force plan**—A well-defined plan to ensure the right sales capability and capacity exists to meet business requirements.

AOE 8: Sales Coaching

Uses sales coaching to develop sales teams and drive sales effectiveness by providing the structured guidance essential for developing sellers; setting clear performance expectations linked to business metrics; developing individualized coaching plans; observing and targeting performance gaps; providing on-the-job reinforcement and corrective feedback; and modeling expected behaviors.

AOE 8: Key Knowledge and Skills

Successful performance requires *knowledge* of:
1. coaching methodology and techniques (both face-to-face and virtually)
2. listening and feedback delivery methods
3. performance critique and debriefing methods
4. performance observation techniques
5. performance review instruments and methods
6. sales excellence practices
7. generational workforce attributes and characteristics.

Successful performance requires the *ability* to:
1. Assess performance objectively.
2. Determine areas for improvement (skills, knowledge, or performance) for individual sales team members.
3. Use a variety of questioning and listening techniques to facilitate self-discovery, learning, motivation, and performance improvement.
4. Build trust with sales team members through connection, competence, and communication.
5. Provide balanced (both positive and constructive) feedback.
6. Assume various roles as needed in role plays to maximize learning (for example, sales person, customer, sales manager, and technical support).
7. Balance performance improvement objectives with a recipient's need for a healthy self-concept.
8. Employ observation to gather the most accurate performance data.
9. Identify "teachable moments" and use them to improve performance.
10. Focus on both the "how" and "what" of performance improvement.

AOE 8: Key Actions

A successful performer:

1. **Creates a climate that facilitates sales coaching**—Builds trust with sales staff, uses effective questioning, works with people on goal setting, and gains agreement on the focus of the coaching sessions.

2. **Observes sales performance to identify opportunities for improvement**—Uses selling opportunities to identify strengths, weaknesses, and opportunities for improvement; ensures that what is observed represents a valid, consistent pattern; and documents observations and conclusions.

3. **Balances corrective feedback with positive feedback to improve performance**—Exploits and leverages teachable moments to ensure individual receptiveness to performance analysis and feedback; provides feedback in a way that recognizes what tasks are performed well; and clearly identifies performance challenges, mistakes made, and provides encouragement for improvement.

4. **Leverages motivation and reward as a key enabler of sales performance**—Seeks to identify individual and team motivators and incorporates them into coaching, leading, reward, and recognition to ensure relevance; actively seeks to remove obstacles to or inhibitors of high motivation.

5. **Connects performance expectations to strategic outcomes**—Ensures that individuals understand how their performance relates to larger organizational or business goals.

6. **Models expected sales behaviors**—Leverages sales experience to model and authentically demonstrate and reinforce sales best practices.

7. **Approaches coaching as a continuous process**—Treats coaching as a process rather than an event and builds on progress made in previous coaching sessions.

8. **Focuses on both results and behaviors**—Sets targets and goals around both results and desired behavior changes.

AOE 8: Sample Outputs

Deliverables include the following:

1. **Coaching strategy**—A game plan and approach, a description of required resources, and timeline for coaching all team members.

2. **Coaching plan**—Observation results (for example, strengths, weaknesses, and opportunities for improvement), planned major coaching activities, and timeline.

3. **Coaching progress report**—Document of progress made on enhancing performance through implementing coaching plan.

4. **Pre-coaching session plan sheets**—A clearly defined set of objectives and activities to provide structure and ensure effective and efficient coaching session.

AOE 9: Sales Talent Selection

Recruits, screens, and hires sales talent by building accurate job descriptions; establishing performance and financial expectations with candidates; collaborating with hiring agencies to recruit the right candidates; managing negotiations with candidates; and supporting the smooth transition of new hires into the organization.

AOE 9: Key Knowledge and Skills

Successful performance requires *knowledge* of:

1. Equal Employment Opportunity Commission (EEOC) laws, regulations, and policy guidance
2. requirements of the sales position (for example, prior experience, company's strategy and type of sale, and desired knowledge and attributes)
3. candidate pipeline management tools
4. company mission, vision, goals, and business strategy
5. linkage between marketing initiatives and sales activities
6. human resources recruitment policies, compliance requirements, and procedures
7. recruitment best practices
8. how to read and interpret sales candidate assessments
9. interviewing methods and strategies (behavioral-based, probing techniques)
10. local, regional, country-level labor laws
11. negotiation methods
12. sales organization or company compensation structure and practices
13. sales or organizational culture and unique requirements
14. employee orientation, education, training, and onboarding
15. succession planning.

Successful performance requires the *ability* to:

1. Build and maintain contacts with colleges and professional recruitment agencies.
2. Use social media (that is, LinkedIn, Facebook, Twitter, etc.) to identify and screen candidates.
3. Use understanding of the requirements of the position to identify, screen, and recruit qualified candidates.
4. Establish candidate relationships based on trust.
5. Influence the definition of job and salary requirements to ensure logical alignment.
6. Validate tacit impressions of a candidate through questioning techniques.
7. Protect the interests of company stakeholders during negotiations.
8. Facilitate new hire transition and integration within the sales organization.

AOE 9: Key Actions

A successful performer:

1. **Develops a solid understanding of the sales organization and sales culture**—Maintains accurate understanding of the sales organization, its composition, history, and challenges, and uses these as reference points when assessing candidates for fit to the organization.

2. **Develops sales position descriptions**—Uses organization's hiring requirements to develop accurate, comprehensive, and enticing position descriptions to attract and identify the right candidates.

3. **Uses a disciplined, systematic, EEOC-compliant process to select sales professionals**—Ensures compliant processes and systems are in place to select sales talent and position sales professionals for success (that is, position postings; sales candidate assessments; selection process steps; offer presentation; position acceptance; start date determination; and new hire requirements for information, technology, tools, and materials).

4. **Aligns and modifies sales job profiles**—Collaborates with stakeholders to enrich standard sales job descriptions; highlights KPIs and supporting skill, knowledge, experience, and attribute requirements; revises and validates job profiles; and sets overall expectations based on clear recruitment objectives and parameters.

5. **Ensures valid compensation packages**—Assesses the compensation package offered for the sales position and job level against industry practices and metrics; works with stakeholders to bring packages into alignment with market standards.

6. **Communicates with sales managers to adjust recruitment goals and job descriptions**—Engages in frequent two-way communication with sales managers/business managers regarding needs and expectations to ensure candidates' skills align with business and market changes.

7. **Monitors and maintains sales candidate pipeline**—Establishes and monitors industry-specific conferences, professional associations, and colleges to identify potential sales candidates; builds candidate lists and continuously updates the pipeline as a basis for sales candidate prospecting.

8. **Contacts, screens, and profiles candidates**—Conducts interviews with potential candidates to determine appropriateness for active candidacy; ensures the accuracy of information and identifies issues requiring further investigation; and creates a short list of potential candidates.

9. **Generates offers and conducts negotiations with sales stakeholders to closure**—Develops and communicates offer letters to candidates; conducts negotiations with candidates to close outstanding gaps (for example, raise benefits and modify requirements); and resolves outstanding issues and processes letter of acceptance.

10. **Supports orientation and onboarding**—Briefs new hires on next steps to ensure a successful transition and integration into the sales organization; maintains constant contact with new hires to troubleshoot problems and ensure onboarding success.

AOE 9: Sample Outputs

Deliverables include the following:

1. **Job/position descriptions**—Descriptions that accurately reflect performance expectations and needed competencies and experiences.

2. **Network of placement resources and contacts**—Accurate and up-to-date list of internal and external recruitment resources, including university placement resources.

3. **Candidate interview data**—A well-documented and objective observation and outcome of interviews with candidates.

4. **Offer letters and cover letters**—Templates that are consistent with company brand and policies and reflect best practices.

5. **Onboarding plan**—A well-defined onboarding plan to ensure speedy integration and improvement of time to productivity.

6. **Sales candidate pipeline of future prospects**—An up-to-date and accurate list of potential candidates with their qualifications for future use.

7. **Sales interview protocols (questions and strategies)**—Situational questions and objective process to accurately assess candidates on business-essential competencies and fit for the job.

8. **EEOC-compliant talent selection process**—A well-defined and documented EEOC-compliant process for identifying, screening, assessing, interviewing, selecting, and communicating with job applicants

9. **Candidate assessment reports**—Documents providing predictive insight into a candidate's sales performance, strengths, potential areas of skill development, and compatibility with the position's requirements.

AOE 10: Sales Talent Development

Develops a high-performing sales team by assessing talent development needs, creating or acquiring learning solutions, delivering and deploying sales training, offering knowledge management opportunities, measuring and evaluating the impact of learning and development solutions, managing or supporting learning management systems, and defining and implementing learning road maps tailored to individual and role-based career paths.

AOE 10: Key Knowledge and Skills

Successful performance requires *knowledge* of:

1. learning style and preferences (individual, cultural, and generational)
2. adult learning principles and practices
3. training needs analysis
4. curriculum and learning road map design
5. blended learning strategies
6. experiential learning methods (for example, work-based learning and on-the-job development techniques—mentoring, job rotation, job shadowing, and case studies)

7. human performance improvement (HPI) principles and practices
8. innovative learning methods (for example, mobile learning, gamification, blended learning, and massive open online course, MOOC), and when to use each to optimize learning
9. sales onboarding best practices
10. learning management systems (LMS)
11. customer relationship management (CRM)
12. learning program evaluation methods (formative and summative)
13. learning program ROI calculation methods
14. test development (item construction/validation)
15. sales competency assessment.

Successful performance requires the *ability* to:

1. Translate business requirements into requirements for learning and development solutions.
2. Conduct learning and development needs analysis.
3. Review and assess individual and role-based learning and development plans.
4. Obtain stakeholders' approval and buy-in on strategic talent development plans and required learning investment.
5. Apply effective delivery and facilitation methods to engage learners and to advance learning.
6. Apply rapid instructional design methods to ensure timely development of learning solutions.
7. Build learning solutions responsive to learner characteristics (for example, learning styles, generational demographics, availability, technical readiness, and cultural norms).
8. Use workplace opportunities to create experiential learning solutions (for example, mentoring, coaching, peer-to-peer tutoring, and case studies).
9. Build valid and reliable tests to measure learning.
10. Select the most appropriate learning approach based on factors such as cost, urgency, and target audience requirements.
11. Implement learning program evaluation systematically to measure the effectiveness and business impact of learning solutions.
12. Leverage learning technologies and platforms to optimize learning.

AOE 10: Key Actions

A successful performer:

1. **Identifies competencies required to achieve the sales strategy**—Identifies business-essential competencies to address performance gaps, achieve business objectives, or meet emerging sales challenges; assesses competency development needs at individual and sales team level.
2. **Conducts sales-learning needs assessments**—Defines sales force learning needs and identifies learning resources, strategies, and solutions needed to address learning needs.

3. **Designs and develops sales talent development solutions**—Partners with subject matter experts (SMEs) to determine the nature, scope, content, and urgency of a sales learning solution; designs learning modules and defines learning paths; and develops learning solutions that resonate with sales audiences, recognize their availability challenges, and speak to their learning preferences.

4. **Delivers learning solutions**—Delivers learning solutions using interactive and effective facilitation techniques to engage the audience and reinforce learning.

5. **Implements and manages deployment of learning programs**—Uses a systematic approach to deploy learning programs in a timely, effective, and efficient manner.

6. **Creates sales onboarding programs**—Develops and deploys new hire orientation and onboarding learning experiences to ensure smooth transition and integration into the sales organization.

7. **Engages, drives, and manages sales audiences**—Generates immediate and compelling interest in the learning event and its value to the sales audience; creates a learning environment that encourages peer discussions, networking, and examples that strengthen transfer of learning; and facilitates small group discussions.

8. **Evaluates sales learning effectiveness and impact**—Evaluates the effectiveness of learning solutions during their formative state and optimizes them prior to full deployment; measures learning transfer and business impact of learning solutions.

9. **Assesses sales competency**—Develops sales competency assessment tools and assesses company gaps at individual, group, and organizational levels.

AOE 10: Sample Outputs

Deliverables include the following:

1. **Sales competency models**—A set of business-essential sales competencies to guide sales talent development.

2. **Sales training needs assessment reports**—A well-defined set of talent development needs and description of requirements for sale learning solutions.

3. **Sales competency gap reports**—Reports on sales competency development needs at individual, sales team, and organizational level.

4. **Learning design plans and specifications**—A blueprint for developing effective learning solutions that articulate expected performance objectives, learning activities, and assessment procedures.

5. **Learning road maps**—Well-defined documents detailing role-based career paths and various levels (entry, intermediate, and advanced) of sales professionals.

6. **Sales or sales-related learning modules**—Consumable learning solutions to be used by the sales force.

7. **Evaluation strategy, plans, and instruments**—A game plan or strategy to evaluate the effectiveness of learning transfer and business impact of the learning solution.

8. **Valid and reliable tests**—Measurable outcomes of the learning solutions.

9. **Learning evaluation reports**—An objective and clear communication of the results of the learning solution evaluation along with recommendations for continuous improvement.

AOE 11: Sales Tool and Process Improvement

Ensures availability of effective sales tools and process by defining, acquiring, and managing sales processes, tools, and systems; incorporating emerging or advanced sales automation in support of business analytics, mobility, and CRM; and maintaining process, tool, or system usability and integrity.

AOE 11: Key Knowledge and Skills

Successful performance requires *knowledge* of:

1. change management methodologies
2. company's sales process, its phases, requirements, and tools
3. CRM systems and the benefits of aligning the sales pipeline component of the CRM to sales process
4. data mining and analysis methods and technology
5. innovative learning delivery systems/media (e-learning, mobile learning, gamification, MOOC, and digital sales playbooks)
6. innovative sales operations productivity tools and technologies (CRM, social media, and mobile applications)
7. quality management tools and processes
8. process analysis and planning methods
9. stakeholders' requirements definition and tracking methods
10. ROI calculation methods and tools
11. KPIs that provide insight into sales force effectiveness using leading and lagging indicators
12. sales operations functions and processes
13. performance support systems, tools, and job aids.

Successful performance requires the *ability* to:

1. Conduct current and future state gap assessment to define requirements for improving sales tools and processes.
2. Educate sales professionals on KPIs, sales process, and benefits of sales process; train sales managers on coaching sales process adherence.
3. Build models depicting all stakeholder interfaces to common tools and applications.
4. Define requirements for and provide needed data and intelligence to all key stakeholders.
5. Manage or support the planning and implementation of innovations.
6. Monitor and assess the value of emerging tools and processes to improve sales productivity and enablement.
7. Identify, select, and manage tools and process improvement vendors.
8. Use the sales pipeline data to identify opportunities for sales process improvement and work with stakeholders to develop a plan of action to improve performance.

AOE 11: Key Actions

A successful performer:

1. **Monitors current sales tools and processes for improvement opportunities—** Assesses current processes, systems, and tools for challenges to productivity, opportunities to automate or integrate functionality, or agile access to sales; identifies gaps and how improvements can enhance sales; and monitors marketplace and vendor offerings for innovations and their appropriateness to meeting company needs.

2. **Develops and drives process/tool planning—** Collaborates with stakeholders and SMEs to identify requirements for tools and process improvement and to create plans to guide infrastructure design and investment decisions.

3. **Educates sales teams on KPIs, processes, and systems—** Collaborates with stakeholders to train sales staff on KPIs, processes, procedures, tools, and systems to drive sales effectiveness throughout the organization.

4. **Creates data and information feed to stakeholders—** Creates, tests, and implements accurate, timely, and usable data, information, and intelligence feed to all key stakeholders.

5. **Manages process/tool upkeep or revision—** Manages revisions of infrastructure solutions to ensure timely rollout and successful implementation; ensures orderly version control and that changes are incorporated in a way that minimizes their impact on the sales function.

6. **Drives or supports sales process/tool change and alignment—** Collaborates with stakeholders in developing and coordinating change programs, communications, and training essential for program readiness and rollout; personally champions and advocates adoption of new systems.

7. **Evaluates impact of process/tool change programs—** Uses sound strategies and methods to evaluate the impact and return on investment of new tools and processes; conducts or supports impact assessments; and ensures the incorporation of results into the improvement of infrastructure initiatives.

AOE 11: Sample Outputs

Deliverables include the following:

1. **Tools/process change requirements document—** An accurate description of business requirement and performance expectation.

2. **Process improvement plan—** A blueprint for enhancing usability, effectiveness, and efficiency of processes along with timeline and needed resources.

3. **Roll-out plan—** A game plan or strategy to roll out a sales process throughout the organization, along with benefits, objectives, timelines, and resource requirements.

4. **Tool/system investment plans—** Required investment and measure of ROI.

5. **Change management plan—** A well-articulated plan to ensure successful implementation and smooth transition to the new process and tool set.

6. **Innovation deployment evaluation report**—An objective report on performance of the new tools and processes and their impact on operational and business metrics.

7. **Tool/system productivity report**—An accurate and objective report on enhanced productivity gained by implementation of the new system/tool.

8. **Standard and regular sales reports**—Available, accessible, and accurate standard sales reports.

9. **Ad hoc report generation capability**—Easy-to-produce, accurate ad hoc sales report.

10. **Training materials**—Education and training materials for all members of the sales ecosystem on how to use tools, processes, and systems to access and use sales productivity data.

AOE 12: Sales Incentive and Compensation Design

Creates and maintains equitable sales compensation and incentive practices to ensure a motivated sales force by researching industry sales compensation metrics; ensuring that compensation and incentive packages reinforce and reward the right sales behaviors in support of the sales strategy; designing and communicating effective incentive campaigns; and measuring the impact of incentive and compensation programs to ensure objectives are met and problems are solved.

AOE 12: Key Knowledge and Skills

Successful performance requires *knowledge* of:

1. compensation research and benchmark sources
2. financial compensation and incentive methods and metrics
3. industry compensation and incentive practices and standards
4. local, regional, and/or country-level regulatory requirements
5. payout processes, key milestones, ratios, and formulas
6. program planning and management skills
7. sales force motivators
8. methods and approaches to measure the business impact of incentive and compensation programs.

Successful performance requires the *ability* to:

1. Build business cases and generate stakeholder buy-in for incentive and compensation programs.
2. Determine competitive yet feasible compensation metrics.
3. Create compelling but flexible and nimble compensation programs proportionate to degree of transformation and change desired.
4. Identify and incorporate market competitive practices into compensation and incentive campaigns.
5. Identify the impact of current and proposed compensation policies on company health and sales force retention or recruiting.

6. Manage compensation change programs.
7. Supplement base payout with innovative reward and recognition strategies.
8. Select, engage, and manage partners and vendors to implement reward and incentive programs (for example, goods and services for incentive campaigns and travel and venues for reward programs).
9. Use software applications for implementing compensation plans.

AOE 12: Key Actions

A successful performer:

1. **Assesses current compensation and incentive programs against best practices—** Identifies compensation challenges unique to sales and researches industry compensation packages, innovations, and competitive advantages; identifies trends or innovations and assesses them for applicability to company challenges.
2. **Aligns compensation and incentive campaigns with business requirements and appropriate sales behaviors and metrics—**Ensures that proposed compensation models and incentive campaigns balance the business strategies with business realities; ensures that compensation aligns with human resource policies, regulatory requirements, and contractual obligations; and ensures that compensation promotes and reinforces productive, high-yield sales behaviors.
3. **Obtains support for sales compensation plans—**Develops and obtains support for sales compensation models that optimize compensation's contribution to a well-motivated sales force.
4. **Drives organizational acceptance of sales compensation changes—**Collaborates with stakeholders in developing change management strategies and programs; develops and coordinates the programs, communications, and awareness training essential for acceptance and successful rollout of changes to the compensation strategy.
5. **Measures business impact of incentive programs—**Measures the business impact of investment made in incentive programs and its contribution to solving problems targeted by these programs.

AOE 12: Sample Outputs

Deliverables include the following:

1. **Sales compensation and incentive research reports—**An accurate and up-to-date summary of competitive and best practices in sales compensation plans and incentive campaigns.
2. **Compensation and incentive plan—**A well-defined, up-to-date, and approved compensation plan that is consistent with company policy and offers appropriate and reasonable local decision making.
3. **Reward and incentive program description—**An accurate and detailed description of reward programs and incentive campaigns (for example, travel, venues, goods, and services) and clear guidelines for implementation.

4. **Compensation communication and training programs**—Materials intended for both members of sales community and hiring managers.

5. **Incentive and compensation impact reports**—Reports on the business impact of incentive programs and recommendations for their continuous improvement.

APPENDIX B

FOUNDATIONAL COMPETENCIES DICTIONARY

The new ATD World-Class Sales Competency Model (WCSCM) defines four clusters of foundational competencies:

1. Collaboration Competencies
2. Insight Competencies
3. Solution Competencies
4. Effectiveness Competencies

Each of these foundational competency clusters includes a number of competencies, as shown Table B-1.

Table B-1: The Four Foundational Competency Clusters

Cluster 1: Collaboration	Cluster 2: Insight
• Relationship Building • Alignment Building • Strategic Partnering • Teaming • Transformational Leadership • Customer Advocacy	• Business and Financial Acumen • Sector/Industry Insight • Evaluating Customer Experiences • Research/Analysis
Cluster 3: Solution	**Cluster 4: Effectiveness**
• Product/Service Acumen • Competitive Intelligence • Consultative Insight • Negotiating and Gaining Commitment • Complex Problem Solving	• Diversity Effectiveness • Global Awareness • Multigenerational Effectiveness • Sales Process Acumen • Technology Fluency • Project Management • Effective Communication • Ethical Decision Making

The following sections describe the *key actions* for all of the competencies in each foundational competency cluster.

Cluster 1: Collaboration Competencies

Sales professionals work interdependently and rely on the following competencies to facilitate these interactions:

- Relationship Building
- Alignment Building
- Strategic Partnering
- Teaming
- Transformational Leadership
- Customer Advocacy.

Relationship Building

Definition: Builds and nurtures positive internal and external relationships to facilitate customer satisfaction, personal effectiveness, and productive collaboration with others.

Key Actions:

- **Actively nurtures positive relationships**—Develops and maintains positive professional relationships among stakeholders, based on personal integrity and trust.
- **Develops and leverages relationships to achieve results**—Strives to build and maintain a network of relationships within and across the organization and leverages the relationships to achieve business results.
- **Protects the integrity of relationships**—Understands the reciprocal nature of relationships and works with others to protect the interests of the larger organization.

Alignment Building

Definition: Works effectively with others across organizational boundaries for the good of the organization.

Key Actions:

- **Positions work meaningfully in terms of its relationship to other functions**—Understands the company's organizational structure, big picture, and the value of cross-organizational collaboration in achieving the goals of the larger enterprise.
- **Advocates collaboration and establishes positive relationships across organizational boundaries**—Sets expectations governing collaboration and minimizes conflict to promote a common focus among all stakeholders.
- **Serves as a role model within the company**—Sets a positive example to peers in other functions by modeling strong interpersonal and relationship building skills.
- **Recognizes and addresses gaps between personal, team, or organizational responsibilities**—Identifies gaps between individual responsibilities and what needs to be accomplished in order to achieve success and takes personal ownership of these areas.

Strategic Partnering

Definition: Actively seeks to understand, align with, and add value to the larger mission of the organization, including the go-to-market strategy.

Key Actions:

- **Maintains a solid understanding of customer challenges**—Stays current with the shifting goals and challenges of the business as the basis for anticipating change and contributing to necessary solutions.
- **Understands the rationale behind strategies and initiatives and actively contributes to their successful implementation**—Takes a broad, cross-organizational perspective on what the business or organization is trying to accomplish and takes steps to help others achieve their goals as easily as possible.
- **Continuously evaluates work in terms of its contribution to meeting business needs**—Critically reviews how work is accomplished within personal area of control for opportunities to better align with business or organizational priorities, meet challenges, or optimize success.

Teaming

Definition: Works effectively in supporting or leading teams to ensure a clear focus, optimum cooperation, and high performance by all team members.

Key Actions:

- **Maintains understanding of effective team processes**—Applies team development and teaming techniques to support teams and encourage team members.
- **Proactively strives to maintain high team performance**—Anticipates opportunities and challenges that affect the team's performance and resolves bottlenecks, communication, other problems or motivational issues that can stand in the way of meeting expectations.
- **Capitalizes on the strengths of individual members to achieve team goals**—Recognizes the different strengths and capabilities of team members and seeks to optimize the fit between individuals and tasks.
- **Operates effectively on virtual teams**—Uses technology and personal skills to overcome proximity challenges to team effectiveness.

Transformational Leadership

Definition: Guides or supports customers through current challenges to optimize the current state and transition to a future desired state.

Key Actions:

- **Drives change and innovation in a way that instills confidence in others**—Eases fears related to change and builds the confidence essential for turning reluctant stakeholders into allies.
- **Provides the mindset critical for implementing continuous improvement and transformation sensitively and effectively**—Exhibits an understanding of the business, organizational, and human behavioral factors that are essential for navigating the challenges involved in transformation and adaption to change.

Customer Advocacy

Definition: Ensures that the concerns and priorities of the customer are understood and addressed, and overall customer satisfaction is achieved.

Key Actions:

- **Ensures customer satisfaction**—Understands how trust and responsiveness to customer needs builds enduring business relationships.
- **Advocates for the customer**—Represents the interests of the customer within company business planning and ensures that a customer-oriented perspective is the touchstone for decision making.

Cluster 2: Insight Competencies

Sales professionals must develop a robust understanding of their customers as well as the skills in information analysis and synthesis needed in order to gather and leverage insight to facilitate and guide customer decision making. The following customer insight competencies are identified within the model:

- Business and Financial Acumen
- Sector/Industry insight
- Evaluating Customer Experiences
- Research/Analysis.

Business and Financial Acumen

Definition: Develops and uses sound business and financial understanding to develop meaningful business recommendations.

Key Actions:

- **Understands what it takes to manage a business**—Uses business and financial acumen to gain solid understanding of customer needs.
- **Applies business insight in opportunity analysis**—Uses insights into customers' KPIs and bigger picture to create, analyze, and qualify opportunities.
- **Positions the financial benefits associated with proposed solution**—Uses financial concepts and techniques to articulate financial return on the proposed solutions (for example, ROI, internal rate of return [IRR], discounted cash flow, total cost of ownership).

Sector/Industry Insight

Definition: Leverages understanding of emerging sector and industry developments as the basis for defining value-added solutions.

Key Actions:

- **Builds reliable sector/industry networks and resources**—Accesses and utilizes relevant sector/industry resources and expertise.
- **Actively monitors the sector/industry landscape for emerging challenges and changes**—Stays current with emerging events (for example, sector, industry, market, technology, regulatory) that may challenge current practices or provide opportunities for practice improvement.

Evaluating Customer Experiences

Definition: Assesses the effectiveness and positive impact of solutions and communicates the results to the stakeholders.

Key Actions:

- **Evaluates the effectiveness and business impact of solutions**—Uses sound methodologies to assess the success of solutions and to identify critical obstacles impacting success.
- **Communicates results in terms of bottom-line business metrics to stakeholders**—Identifies and uses key business or operational metrics that clearly express beneficial results that are understood and valued by stakeholders (for example, net promoter scores, total cost of ownership, ROI, and productivity ratios).

Research/Analysis

Definition: Proactively and systematically collects information needed for effective decision making, planning, relationship building, and well-targeted solutions.

Key Actions:

- **Determines the range, type, and scope of information needed**—Systematically assesses problems, challenges, and opportunities to ensure that the right sources are utilized and that critical information is collected.
- **Applies the most appropriate tools and strategies to gather needed information**—Understands which tools and strategies are best suited for collecting needed information.
- **Incorporates information effectively into action**—Ensures that information informs decisions or activities in a timely manner and in a way that is relevant, supports the weighing of options, and adds value.

Cluster 3: Solution Competencies

Sales professionals must develop strategies for identifying the right solution, generating enthusiasm for the solution they propose, competitively positioning it, and negotiating and gaining commitment. The following competencies are identified in the model:

- Product/Service Acumen
- Competitive Intelligence
- Consultative Insight
- Negotiating and Gaining Commitment
- Complex Problem Solving.

Product/Service Acumen

Definition: Demonstrates a solid understanding of the company's products and services and their value proposition.

Key Actions:

- **Maintains a solid understanding of product/service offerings**—Understands the company's products, services, and solutions at a level appropriate to work responsibilities and sufficient to build credibility with other stakeholders.

- **Understands solution components and how they add value**—Understands how solutions can best be applied or adapted to address business or organizational needs.

Competitive Intelligence

Definition: Applies competitive insight to effectively differentiate and position solutions.
Key Actions:

- **Stays current with the competitive landscape**—Maintains an understanding of the competitive landscape and the strengths and weaknesses of competitor offerings.
- **Ensures that competitor claims are appropriately vetted in solution definition and planning**—Applies competitive intelligence as a critical component of sales or account support to ensure effective messaging.
- **Understands competitor's strategies and tactics**—Uses knowledge of competitor to develop strategies and counter-tactics to sell competitively.

Consultative Insight

Definition: Provides the informed experience, breadth of insight, and robust exploration essential for helping customers to make an optimum decision.
Key Actions:

- **Challenges the customer by providing a wider perspective to solution definition**—Ensures that solution definition takes into account the broader context of trends, developments, and opportunities that should factor into decision making.
- **Ensures that solutions are justified and in the best interest of the customer**—Effectively communicates solution alternatives and their impact on solving business challenges as the basis for determining the best course of action.
- **Ensures that the proposed solutions satisfy customer needs**—Works with customers to identify any contingencies that may pose risks to what the customer seeks to achieve in deployment.
- **Maintains involvement in online communities**—Establishes visibility through various media to keep current with emerging best practices.

Negotiating and Gaining Commitment

Definition: Helps align all stakeholder interests to create a win/win balance that demonstrates mutual benefit, increases the probability of commitment, and drives the opportunity to closure.
Key Actions:

- **Effectively plans and prepares for negotiations**—Defines a negotiation strategy and prepares the negotiating team for successful implementation of the strategy.
- **Determines optimum bargaining position**—Defines valid expectation and desired outcomes and identifies walk-away position.
- **Builds value propositions**—Identifies key decision makers' criteria for success and aligns the solution to these criteria to gain buy-in from multiple stakeholders.

- **Applies appropriate techniques to reach agreements**—Gains commitment and closes the deal by interpreting signals accurately, emphasizing critical points, and providing needed justification.

Complex Problem Solving

Definition: Creatively brings new or alternative perspectives forward for consideration in order to overcome complex challenges.

Key Actions:

- **Approaches challenges creatively**—Demonstrates forward thinking, reconceptualizes challenges to explore alternative possibilities, and exploits opportunities to enhance or improve results.
- **Crosses disciplines to frame or address challenges**—Works outside of comfort zone and draws from multiple disciplines or models to synthesize new approaches to problem solving.

Cluster 4: Effectiveness Competencies

Given the accelerating change and dynamic nature of the sales environment, individuals must demonstrate personal professional effectiveness and responsibility. The following competencies are identified in the model:

- Diversity Effectiveness
- Global Awareness
- Multigenerational Effectiveness
- Sales Process Acumen
- Technology Fluency
- Project Management
- Effective Communication
- Ethical Decision Making.

Diversity Effectiveness

Definition: Values diversity (gender, ethnic, racial, and cultural) and effectively leverages the insights and experiences of others to achieve goals and establish a stimulating, productive work environment.

Key Actions:

- **Demonstrates respect for others**—Respects the innate human dignity of every individual and conscientiously avoids language or actions that might prove offensive or derogatory.
- **Adapts to diverse work settings**—Demonstrates an appreciation of diverse perspectives and approaches to work and actively seeks to listen, learn, and integrate different ways of doing things into the workplace.
- **Harnesses diversity to create workplace synergies**—Leverages the experiences and worldviews of others to drive innovations and stimulate creativity.

Global Awareness

Definition: Understands the interconnectedness of modern business and works effectively within the global workplace.

Key Actions:

- **Incorporates a global perspective to accommodate others**—Where warranted by a project's scope, makes decisions within a global context that is sensitive to local considerations (for example, culture, law, rules and regulations).
- **Ensures the effectiveness of global communications**—Applies appropriate communication style and language to suit cultural, social, and linguistic differences so that a message is delivered correctly and professionally.
- **Adapts tactics to maintain the momentum of global initiatives**—Demonstrates reliability and adaptability in meeting the challenges of working within global time zones.

Multigenerational Effectiveness

Definition: Understands intergenerational differences and appro aches work-related interactions based on these differences to ensure optimum results.

Key Actions:

- **Develops a solid understanding of generational differences as the basis for effective interaction**—Builds and maintains understanding of the key characteristics that differentiate generations (for example, adeptness with technology, motivating influences, work habits, and communication styles/preferences).
- **Builds and incorporates the tactics critical for working effectively with generational differences**—Adapts and applies best practices in working with multigenerational teams to achieve desired results.

Sales Process Acumen

Definition: Demonstrates a solid understanding of company's selling process and aligns personal activities to the prescribed roles and responsibilities in the selling process.

Key Actions:

- **Maintains a solid understanding of sales methodology**—Maintains an up-to-date knowledge of the sales process, including phases, major activities, outcomes, exit criteria, and roles and responsibilities.
- **Aligns and relates work to sales process**—Executes the selling behaviors and tasks essential for successful prospecting, qualifying, proposing, negotiating, and closing on deals.

Technology Fluency

Definition: Understands the contributions that technology makes to optimizing productivity and actively incorporates technology into work processes.

Key Actions:

- **Understands how technology supports optimum performance and seeks to master tool or system innovations**—Readily adapts to technical innovations and actively seeks to master the skills and knowledge required for their effective application.
- **Effectively incorporates technology into work**—Uses technology effectively to expedite activities, ensure responsiveness, and facilitate job effectiveness (enhance connectivity, accelerate learning, execute research and data manipulation, present information, track developments, and speed up reporting).
- **Embraces personal productivity technology**—Takes the initiative to learn new technology and incorporate its benefits into the workplace (for example, customer relationship management [CRM] systems, virtual learning, social media, and mobile communication devices).

Project Management

Definition: Applies basic project management methods to ensure the successful progress of critical tasks.

Key Actions:

- **Organizes and manages work systematically**—Uses project management techniques to define requirements, control scope, track and manage costs and time, and so on.
- **Organizes and manages resources effectively**—Identifies and monitors people, funding, and resources to ensure cost-effective project or program results.
- **Adaptively applies methods as needed to achieve goals**—Makes necessary adjustments as requirements change or new ones emerge.

Effective Communication

Definition: Prepares clear, concise, and persuasive customer and internal communications, demonstrating effective writing and presentations skills and active listening, and projecting a credible image.

Key Actions:

- **Listens actively**—Pays close attention to what is being said and uses questioning techniques effectively to probe and clarify in pursuit of accurate understanding.
- **Achieves communication objectives**—Ensures that verbal and written communications and group presentations are well-prepared, clear, concise, accurate, and persuasive.
- **Communicates persuasively**—Influences perceptions and uses sound reasoning to achieve desired responses or decisions.
- **Uses Storytelling**—Uses business cases and references to tell compelling and persuasive stories.

Ethical Decision Making

Definition: Adheres to ethical standards of personal conduct and business rules when making decisions or executing tasks.

Key Actions:

- **Demonstrates personal integrity**—Takes personal responsibility for ensuring that actions and decisions protect the integrity of the company and contribute to a valued environment of practice.
- **Incorporates quality considerations into decision making**—Determines the best course of action in compliance with established quality processes, business rules, or optimum workplace practices.

APPENDIX C

RESEARCH METHODOLOGY

Purpose

The goal of updating the original ATD World-Class Sales Competency Model (WCSCM) was not just to revise the original 13 sales areas of expertise (AOEs) and foundational competencies but to do so in a way that ensured that the new WCSCM would:

- Reflect the trends that are shaping the sales profession.
- Encompass current and emerging sales practices to create a model that is relevant both today and in the next few years.
- Be relevant across various job titles in the sales organization and sales enablement functions.
- Include the perspectives of sales professionals as well as employers.
- Be actionable, easy to navigate, and accurate, so as to be used for a variety of sales talent management efforts, such as recruitment, selection, assessment, and development.

Only a robust study could ensure such results.

Approach

To create the new ATD WCSCM, the project team followed a three-phase process: planning, revising, and validating. A description of the goals and major activities of each research phase follows (Figure C-1).

Figure C-1: Flowchart of the Three Research Phases and Major Activities

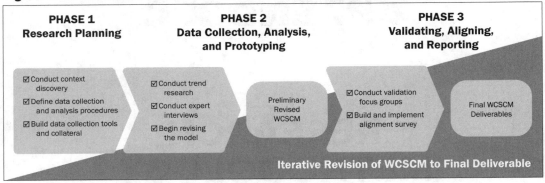

Phase 1. Research Planning

The goal of this phase was to create a research plan by defining data collection and analysis procedures and developing tools. Included were the following activities:

- Define and finalize the research requirements.
- Specify an implementation plan and timeline that includes major activities with designated individuals responsible for the activities.
- Identify key WCSCM sales populations and stakeholders targeted and served by the WCSCM.
- Define a set of criteria and guidelines for project contributors. One of the goals of the research was to revise the model by obtaining input from sales professionals worldwide and in various industries. Therefore, every effort was made to ensure a global and cross-industry perspective by selecting worldwide samples representing various industries to participate in the one-on-one interviews, validation focus groups, and role alignment survey.
- Start the process of identifying and recruiting sales thought leaders and sales practitioners to participate in interviews and validation focus groups and survey efforts.
- Build data collection and analysis tools and templates.

Phase 2. Data Collection, Analysis, and Prototyping

The goal of this phase was to prepare a preliminary draft of the new WCSCM based on a range of data collection and analysis activities, including literature review, the market pulse survey, and SME/stakeholder input. This phase was completed in the following three steps:

- Step 2.1 Conducting trend analysis
- Step 2.2 Collecting input from sales thought leaders and leading sales practitioners
- Step 2.3 Drafting the preliminary version of the revised WCSCM.

Step 2.1. Conducting Trend Analysis

The objective of this step was to conduct a sales trends literature review to identify emerging trends and sales practices that are shaping the sales profession. Included were the following activities:

- Scan and obtain a wide range of documents and collateral describing emerging sales trends.
- Conduct a trend analysis to determine forces shaping the sales profession and recent developments in sales practices since the WCSCM was developed in 2008.

Step 2.2. Collecting SME Input

The objective of this step was to obtain input from thought leaders and leading sales practitioners worldwide in various industries to revise the WCSCM. Activities included the following:

- Schedule interviews with a select group of thought leaders and leading sales practitioners worldwide in various industries.
- Conduct one-on-one interviews. Each interview lasted approximately 45 minutes and focused on a set of core questions to determine:
- Emerging sales practices
- Challenges faced by sales professionals in their areas of expertise and/or organizational context, desired behaviors to overcome those challenges, and needed competencies that fuel those behaviors
- Recommendations for revising and reconfiguring the AOEs and their content (for example, key knowledge and skills, key actions, and sample outputs).

Step 2.3. Drafting the Preliminary Version of the New WCSCM

The objective of this step was to prepare a complete draft of the new WCSCM; it involved the following activities:

- Analyze and utilize the results of trend literature analysis.
- Analyze and utilize the results of interviews conducted with SMEs.
- Populate the new structure of the AOEs with the insights gained from trend literature review and SME interviews.
- Develop a WCSCM change-tracking document that identifies content and structural changes and that lists references for additional information on new concepts or topics added.
- Share the preliminary model with project stakeholders to obtain feedback and to revise the draft of the revised WCSCM.

Phase 3. Validation, Alignment, and Reporting

The goal of this phase was to ensure an actionable, relevant, and accurate WCSCM. This included validation, role alignment, finalization, and reporting of the new WCSCM, based on data collected in the second phase of the study. This phase was completed in the following two steps:

- Step 3.1 Validate the New Model
- Step 3.2 Set Relative Importance of AOEs Through WCSCM Role Alignment.

Step 3.1. Validate the New Model

The objective of this step was to use focus groups and one-on-one reviews to validate the new model developed in the previous phases. Included were the following activities:

- Work with the advisory team to recruit the knowledgeable people identified in Phase 1 to review the revised WCSCM.
- Draft a set of guidelines for facilitation of the focus groups.
- Prepare review packages (including the new model and review guidelines) for reviewers.
- Complete the focus groups and individual review sessions and analyze the input.
- Revise the new WCSCM based on focus group feedback.

Step 3.2. Set Relative Importance of AOEs Through WCSCM Role Alignment

The objectives of this step were to:

- Further validate the revised WCSCM and related information collected in previous phases.
- Determine the relative importance of sales profession competencies for various roles and for various sales contexts (for example, market segments, industry verticals, product/service/solution sets).
- Revise and finalize the new WCSCM.

Activities included the following:

- Develop a WCSCM role alignment and relevance survey.
- Identify appropriate demographics to select the survey sample.
- Implement the survey using the ATD survey system.
- Analyze the results and capture the relative importance of the competencies for various roles and sales contexts.
- Update and finalize the revised WCSCM.

APPENDIX D

VALIDATION SURVEY RESULTS— DEMOGRAPHICS AND SUMMARY

Part 1: Demographics

The following tables show demographics of the respondents to the World-Class Sales Competency Model (WCSCM) survey.

Region

Respondents identified the region in which they were based.

Regions	%
Asia/Pacific (including China, SE Asia, India, and Australia/New Zealand)	8.9%
Europe (including European Union and Russia)	9.2%
Middle East/Africa	1.4%
Central and Latin America	5.8%
North America (including Canada and United States)	74.7%

Sales Roles

The following roles best characterize respondents' current jobs (regardless of the titles they currently hold). If more than one role was valid, they were asked to pick their primary role.

Job Title	%
Sales Management and Leadership	
Sales Executive (senior level sales management and oversight of selling organization and associated resources)	15.1%
Sales Manager (management of salespeople and budget; resource and personnel alignment, etc.)	4.0%
Sales Specialist Manager	1.5%
Presales Managers	0.0%
Channel/Partner Sales Managers	1.5%
Sales Force	
Sales Representative (account manager, territory manager, account executive)	8.5%
Sales Specialist (selling aligned with specific product/service or sales support)	1.1%
Presales Consultant (aligned with sales as a technical consultant or solution designer)	1.8%
Channel/Partner Account Manager	0.0%
Sales Enablement	
Sales Enablement Manager (ops manager, compensation manager, recruitment manager, etc.)	4.0%
Enablement Executive (director or vice president of sales operations, compensation, etc.)	3.7%
Sales Compensation Planner	0.0%
Sales Operations Infrastructure Developer	0.4%
Sales Operations Researcher or Analyst	0.7%
Sales Recruiter	0.0%
Sales Development	7.7%
Sales Training Manager	13.6%
Sales Training Executive (director, vice president)	5.5%
Sales Trainer, Coach, or Consultant (sales instructor, facilitator, sales consultant, sales coach)	16.5%
Sales Training Designer and Developer	11.4%
Sales Researcher	2.2%
Professor/Academic	0.7%

Time in Role

Respondents indicated the amount of time in their current role.

Years	%
Less Than 1 year	10.4%
Between 1 and 3 years	19.4%
Between 3 and 5 years	18.1%
Between 6 and 10 years	19.4%
Between 11 and 15 years	12.2%
More Than 15 years	20.5%

Industry

Respondents identified the industry for their own respective organization.

Industry	%
Construction	0.3%
Consulting	16.4%
Education	6.5%
Energy	0.7%
Financial Services	10.6%
Government (nonmilitary, noneducational)	1.4%
Military	0.0%
Healthcare	9.9%
Manufacturing	8.2%
Nonprofit	1.7%
Raw material production	0.0%
Real Estate	0.7%
Retail	2.4%
Technology	13.0%
Training and development-related products and services	14.7%
Other (e.g., insurance, transportation, advertising, hospitality, food and beverage, or auto repair)	13.4%
Don't Know	0.0%

*The "other" category also included several responses such as telecommunications that could have been categorized by the technology industry.

Age

Respondents indicated their age range.

Age	%
29 or less	3.8%
30-39	18.5%
40-49	30.5%
50-59	31.2%
60 or above	16.1%

Gender

Respondents indicated their gender.

Gender	%
Male	55.7%
Female	44.3%

Membership

Respondents indicated whether they were a member of ATD.

ATD Member	%
Yes	62.7%
No	37.3%

Respondents indicated whether they were a member of ATD Sales Enablement Community.

ATD Sales Enablement	%
Yes	26.5%
No	73.5%

Respondents indicated whether they considered themselves to be part of the sales profession.

Sales Profession	%
Yes	64.4%
No	35.6%

Respondents indicated whether they were part of the training and development profession.

Training and Development Profession	%
Yes	93.1%
No	6.9%

Part 2: Sales Areas of Expertise (AOE) Validation

In this section we asked respondents to rate the importance of *key actions, knowledge areas, and skills* in each Sales AOE critical to their success, using the following 5-point scale.

    5—Critical (It is crucial to my success.)
    4—Very Important (It is important.)
    3—Moderate Importance (It has a moderate level of importance.)
    2—Slightly Important (It has some importance to my success.)
    1—Not at all important (It has little or no importance to my success.)

AOE 1: New Account Acquisition

How important are the following key **actions** for effective performance?

New Account Acquisition: Key Actions	Critical (5)	Very important (4)	Moderately important (3)	Slightly important (2)	Not at all important (1)	Mean
Establishes a social media presence as a credible source of information worth following	15%	23%	29%	25%	8%	3.13
Uses social media to create new customer networks	12%	29%	31%	17%	12%	3.12
Researches and targets prospects	54%	29%	13%	2%	2%	4.31
Initiates interest-building engagements	50%	35%	8%	8%	0%	4.27
Qualifies prospects	50%	37%	12%	0%	2%	4.33
Develops winning proposals	61%	25%	10%	2%	2%	4.41
Negotiates deals and drives opportunities to close	69%	20%	8%	2%	2%	4.51
Follows company's sales process	22%	41%	27%	6%	4%	3.71
Pursues global sales opportunities	12%	33%	24%	12%	20%	3.06

How important are the following key **knowledge areas** for effective performance?

New Account Acquisition: Key Knowledge	Critical (5)	Very important (4)	Moderately important (3)	Slightly important (2)	Not at all important (1)	Mean
Product/service features, drawbacks, benefits, and value propositions	62%	37%	2%	0%	0%	4.60
Prospect business and financial health information, including key performance indicators (KPIs)	29%	45%	16%	8%	2%	3.92
Resource knowledge (e.g., marketing/industry, technical, pricing, legal, delivery, and fulfillment)	33%	48%	19%	0%	0%	4.13
Lead generation and management procedures	35%	33%	25%	4%	4%	3.90
Hunting and opportunity discovery techniques and best practices	42%	38%	12%	6%	2%	4.13
Objection and drawbacks handling techniques	31%	48%	17%	4%	0%	4.06
Competitive analysis and positioning resources	25%	45%	27%	2%	0%	3.94
Opportunity qualification and sizing techniques	29%	44%	19%	6%	2%	3.92
Sales cycle management techniques	16%	39%	35%	4%	6%	3.55
Social media sites and connectivity applications	8%	17%	38%	29%	8%	2.88
Company's selling process	23%	33%	33%	10%	2%	3.65
Company's core competencies	46%	35%	15%	4%	0%	4.23
Company's pricing guidelines, including discount and approval process	35%	31%	23%	8%	4%	3.85
Customer relationship management best practices	21%	44%	21%	8%	6%	3.67
Buyers' business challenges and their drivers	60%	35%	4%	0%	2%	4.50
Business standards of conduct and ethical business practices	53%	32%	11%	2%	2%	4.32

How important are the following key **skills** for effective performance?

New Account Acquisition: Key Skills	Critical (5)	Very important (4)	Moderately important (3)	Slightly important (2)	Not at all important (1)	Mean
Define engagement strategies based on assessment of prospects and their likelihood to buy	53%	32%	11%	2%	2%	4.32
Adjust engagement tactics based on a careful reading of a prospect's receptiveness	51%	38%	9%	2%	0%	4.38
Execute hunting and opportunity discovery efforts with persistence in the face of rejection	49%	28%	15%	8%	0%	4.19
Engage prospects in an exploratory conversation about their needs by focusing on listening, analyzing the information, summarizing their needs to confirm understanding, and avoiding a direct sales pitch	72%	25%	4%	0%	0%	4.68
Leverage market and industry insights accurately when positioning offers	40%	49%	11%	0%	0%	4.28
Manage leads and ensure follow-up/follow-through	64%	25%	9%	2%	0%	4.51
Map prospect management structure and decision-making authority	32%	47%	17%	0%	4%	4.04
Track and manage multiple sales opportunities and prospect engagements	51%	25%	19%	6%	0%	4.21
Identify the prospect's purchase drivers (e.g., needs, priorities, problems to be solved, or opportunities to be realized)	74%	23%	4%	0%	0%	4.70
Adapt and deliver sales presentations that speak to the prospect's most urgent needs	49%	40%	11%	0%	0%	4.38
Follow the sales process and utilize integrated CRM systems to manage and advance opportunities to closure and provide complete, accurate, and timely information	26%	36%	25%	9%	4%	3.72
Pursue global sales opportunities with sensitivity to cultural differences	15%	30%	19%	15%	21%	3.04
Present value propositions in compelling stories	53%	40%	4%	2%	2%	4.40
Identify issues that might require a need to modify the sales approach	52%	37%	12%	0%	0%	4.40

AOE 2: Account Development and Retention

How important are the following key **actions** for effective performance?

Account Development and Retention: Key Actions	Critical (5)	Very important (4)	Moderately important (3)	Slightly important (2)	Not at all important (1)	Mean
Develops and maintains strategic account plans	39%	37%	13%	9%	2%	4.02
Gathers and maintains account intelligence	39%	41%	20%	0%	0%	4.20
Actively targets and shapes customer business planning	35%	41%	15%	9%	0%	4.02
Maintains customer satisfaction and resolves customer complaints	61%	37%	2%	0%	0%	4.59
Builds, nurtures, and extends client business relationships	72%	22%	7%	0%	0%	4.65
Cultivates and achieves trusted advisor status	63%	37%	0%	0%	0%	4.63
Protects and expands accounts	50%	39%	4%	4%	2%	4.30
Uses CRM as a tool to maintain account information	22%	33%	28%	9%	9%	3.50
Collaborates with multinational sales and customer teams	15%	35%	15%	13%	22%	3.09

How important are the following key **knowledge areas** for effective performance?

Account Development and Retention: Key Knowledge	Critical (5)	Very important (4)	Moderately important (3)	Slightly important (2)	Not at all important (1)	Mean
Account farming procedures and best practices—cultivating opportunities within existing accounts (e.g., check-ins, sponsoring marketing initiatives)	39%	35%	17%	4%	4%	4.00
Account history and contacts (prior investments, account relationships)	30%	41%	24%	4%	0%	3.98
Account planning tools, templates, and procedures	17%	30%	35%	13%	4%	3.43
Business metrics (e.g., health ratios, return on investment (ROI), total cost of ownership)	28%	22%	33%	9%	9%	3.52
Rules of engagement, rewards, and commission structure regarding win-backs	9%	33%	30%	17%	11%	3.11
Competitive information resources	30%	35%	20%	13%	2%	3.78
Contract administration and renewal processes and resources	22%	24%	37%	11%	7%	3.43
Customer-oriented vertical industry information resources (e.g., Dun & Bradstreet, analyst reports)	15%	22%	24%	26%	13%	3.00
Back-office administrative/ order-entry procedures	11%	28%	33%	20%	9%	3.13
Product/service features, benefits, and value propositions	46%	41%	11%	2%	0%	4.30
Supply chain knowledge (lead times, response rates, global fulfillment processes)	17%	43%	24%	2%	13%	3.50
Client's businesses life cycle (e.g., start-up, growth, maintain phase)	41%	28%	15%	11%	4%	3.91

How important are the following key **skills** for effective performance?

Account Development and Retention: Key Skills	Critical (5)	Very important (4)	Moderately important (3)	Slightly important (2)	Not at all important (1)	Mean
Acquire and manage leads and referrals	57%	26%	9%	7%	2%	4.28
Develop, manage, and modify long-term sales strategies	50%	33%	13%	0%	4%	4.24
Coordinate and align all account activities within the account plan	41%	35%	17%	0%	7%	4.04
Apply sales process and pipeline management practices, tools, metrics, and policies to prioritize and manage selling	24%	43%	22%	4%	7%	3.74
Calculate business metrics and translate product/service features into value propositions	28%	41%	24%	0%	7%	3.85
Effectively engage and partner with customer executives and key functions (e.g., purchasing)	57%	24%	15%	2%	2%	4.30
Collaborate with procurement to show promised savings or efficiencies	30%	35%	20%	2%	13%	3.67
Leverage marketing programs to advance sales	17%	30%	39%	9%	4%	3.48
Leverage contract administration and renewal opportunities for up-selling and cross-selling	26%	24%	35%	9%	7%	3.54
Manage total customer satisfaction to optimize relationships	63%	28%	9%	0%	0%	4.54
Set accurate customer expectations for order fulfillment (e.g., lead times, response rates, fulfillment processes)	46%	30%	13%	2%	9%	4.02
Translate competitive knowledge into relevant competitive countering messages	28%	41%	22%	4%	4%	3.85
Leverage testimonials and references from other customers to retain and grow the account	37%	35%	17%	9%	2%	3.96
Collaborate with account teams in various countries in global accounts	13%	33%	17%	13%	24%	2.98

AOE 3: Complex Solution Definition and Positioning

How important are the following key **actions** for effective performance?

Complex Solution Definition and Positioning: Key Actions	Critical (5)	Very important (4)	Moderately important (3)	Slightly important (2)	Not at all important (1)	Mean
Performs technical qualifications	15%	38%	38%	4%	4%	3.55
Designs complex solutions	30%	40%	26%	4%	0%	3.96
Customizes standard products or services	30%	35%	26%	7%	2%	3.85
Conducts technical demonstrations and benchmarks	15%	30%	40%	13%	2%	3.43
Sizes complex solutions	23%	34%	36%	4%	2%	3.72
Articulates solution designs	49%	30%	17%	4%	0%	4.23
Defines deployment options	30%	41%	24%	4%	0%	3.98

How important are the following key **knowledge areas** for effective performance?

Complex Solution Definition and Positioning: Key Knowledge	Critical (5)	Very important (4)	Moderately important (3)	Slightly important (2)	Not at all important (1)	Mean
Complex opportunity qualification techniques	30%	34%	23%	11%	2%	3.79
Product/service/solution technology (e.g., concepts, uses)	26%	53%	17%	4%	0%	4.00
Business context and business impact of complex solutions	45%	36%	13%	4%	2%	4.17
Requirements analysis and management techniques	26%	38%	28%	6%	2%	3.79
Solution design methodologies, best practices, and trends	30%	38%	23%	4%	4%	3.85
Solution configuration frameworks or templates	22%	37%	33%	7%	2%	3.70
Solution design procedures and communication conventions (written/visual)	32%	36%	21%	9%	2%	3.87
Solution sizing criteria	11%	48%	28%	9%	4%	3.52
Technical trust-building and selling	49%	32%	13%	4%	2%	4.21
Sales process phases and at what phase in the process a solution is defined and positioned	30%	38%	21%	9%	2%	3.85

How important are the following key **skills** for effective performance?

Complex Solution Definition and Positioning: Key Skills	Critical (5)	Very important (4)	Moderately important (3)	Slightly important (2)	Not at all important (1)	Mean
Define detailed solution requirements	36%	47%	15%	2%	0%	4.17
Translate solution designs into meaningful customer benefits and align them to stakeholder needs	66%	34%	0%	0%	0%	4.66
Competitively position product or service and articulate its value in tangible or measurable terms	53%	34%	9%	4%	0%	4.36
Develop trusted advisor status with customers by demonstrating solution acumen	60%	40%	0%	0%	0%	4.60
Communicate technical solutions to nontechnical audiences	40%	36%	17%	4%	2%	4.09
Ensure cost-effective solution deployment and delivery practices	32%	47%	19%	2%	0%	4.09
Manage technical teams and integrate their contributions	19%	34%	21%	15%	11%	3.36
Adhere to sales process phases to ensure that the steps leading up to defining and positioning a solution have been completed	26%	33%	28%	7%	7%	3.65

AOE 4: Partner Sales Support

How important are the following key **actions** for effective performance?

Partner Sales Support: Key Actions	Critical (5)	Very important (4)	Moderately important (3)	Slightly important (2)	Not at all important (1)	Mean
Drives joint sales planning and forecasting	30%	60%	10%	0%	0%	4.20
Assesses and ensures partner's sales force readiness	40%	50%	10%	0%	0%	4.30
Motivates and educates partners	80%	10%	10%	0%	0%	4.70
Cultivates partner business relationships	70%	30%	0%	0%	0%	4.70
Facilitates inventory balancing/clearance	30%	0%	20%	30%	20%	2.90
Tracks investments in partner selling to determine business impact	30%	40%	30%	0%	0%	4.00
Troubleshoots partner sales crediting	30%	20%	30%	20%	0%	3.60
Collaborates in team selling and positioning	56%	44%	0%	0%	0%	4.56

How important are the following key **knowledge areas** for effective performance?

Partner Sales Support: Key Knowledge	Critical (5)	Very important (4)	Moderately important (3)	Slightly important (2)	Not at all important (1)	Mean
Company indirect sales motion, strategy, and direction	40%	40%	20%	0%	0%	4.20
Rules of engagement with partners	50%	40%	10%	0%	0%	4.40
Partner business model and financial health	40%	60%	0%	0%	0%	4.40
Partner incentive programs	40%	60%	0%	0%	0%	4.40
Procedures for escalating and resolving partner issues	30%	50%	10%	10%	0%	4.00
Partner loyalty and commitment-building techniques	56%	44%	0%	0%	0%	4.56
Partner sales crediting processes and tools	30%	30%	30%	10%	0%	3.80
Partner types and functions (distributors, resellers, specialized partners)	33%	11%	33%	22%	0%	3.56
Sell-with, sell-through, sell-for techniques	40%	40%	20%	0%	0%	4.20
Partner skill requirements and certification processes	40%	20%	30%	0%	10%	3.80
Partner's selling process	Not analyzed in raw data					

How important are the following key **skills** for effective performance?

Partner Sales Support: Key Skills	Critical (5)	Very important (4)	Moderately important (3)	Slightly important (2)	Not at all important (1)	Mean
Prepare joint business plans	40%	40%	10%	10%	0%	4.10
Enhance partner commitment and gain share of partner wallet	80%	10%	0%	10%	0%	4.60
Set service level agreement expectations with partners	40%	40%	20%	0%	0%	4.20
Expedite partner reporting and communications using automated tools (e.g., CRM)	20%	40%	30%	10%	0%	3.70
Ensure partner compliance to product or service certification requirements	40%	30%	20%	0%	10%	3.90
Ensure timely and accurate product/service updates to partners	40%	50%	10%	0%	0%	4.30
Implement partner performance assessments	40%	30%	20%	10%	0%	4.00
Influence operations to ensure timely and accurate payout to partners	40%	30%	20%	10%	0%	4.00
Leverage marketing programs and initiatives to advance partner selling	30%	40%	30%	0%	0%	4.00

AOE 5: Sales Pipeline and Forecast Management

How important are the following key **actions** for effective performance?

Sales Pipeline and Forecast Management: Key Actions	Critical (5)	Very important (4)	Moderately important (3)	Slightly important (2)	Not at all important (1)	Mean
Harnesses CRM to achieve sales objectives	40%	27%	27%	7%	0%	4.00
Develops and manages accurate sales pipelines	38%	38%	25%	0%	0%	4.13
Develops accurate sales forecasts and reports	56%	19%	25%	0%	0%	4.31
Sets competitive pricing and protects margin	50%	25%	25%	0%	0%	4.25

How important are the following key **knowledge areas** for effective performance?

Sales Pipeline and Forecast Management: Key Knowledge	Critical (5)	Very important (4)	Moderately important (3)	Slightly important (2)	Not at all important (1)	Mean
Sales process, process stages, and requirements to advance from one stage to the next	44%	31%	19%	0%	6%	4.06
Big data-enabled analytics to manage the pipeline more effectively	25%	38%	25%	6%	6%	3.69
CRM systems and tools	38%	31%	25%	6%	0%	4.00
Forecast discipline and associated methods/processes	31%	31%	25%	6%	6%	3.75
Forecast report templates and requirements	25%	38%	19%	13%	6%	3.63
Margin management requirements and techniques	19%	38%	13%	19%	13%	3.31
Sales analytics methods	19%	44%	19%	13%	6%	3.56
Company's pricing guidelines, including discount and approval process	25%	44%	25%	0%	6%	3.81
Financial basics (e.g., balance sheet, income statement, cash flow statement)	19%	25%	25%	6%	25%	3.06

How important are the following key **skills** for effective performance?

Sales Pipeline and Forecast Management: Key Skills	Critical (5)	Very important (4)	Moderately important (3)	Slightly important (2)	Not at all important (1)	Mean
Apply relevant account planning tools, templates, and procedures	25%	44%	25%	0%	6%	3.81
Manage and assess the quality, size, shape, and velocity of the sales pipeline	31%	50%	13%	6%	0%	4.06
Prepare accurate and timely sales forecasts	31%	56%	6%	6%	0%	4.13
Use margin requirements when qualifying opportunities and prospects to ensure profitability	19%	38%	38%	0%	6%	3.63
Build a sales pipeline of high-quality opportunities and disqualify unlikely and poorly fit opportunities	44%	38%	13%	6%	0%	4.19
Use CRM systems to enter relevant information for forecasting, resource allocation, and decision making	38%	31%	25%	6%	0%	4.00
Conduct win-loss analysis and share insights with other stakeholders	19%	31%	25%	19%	6%	3.38

AOE 6: Sales Strategy Definition and Execution

How important are the following key **actions** for effective performance?

Sales Strategy Definition and Execution: Key Actions	Critical (5)	Very important (4)	Moderately important (3)	Slightly important (2)	Not at all important (1)	Mean
Assesses the effectiveness of the current sales strategy	60%	35%	5%	0%	0%	4.55
Identifies and promotes effective and innovative sales practices	35%	55%	10%	0%	0%	4.25
Creates strategic sales plans	45%	40%	15%	0%	0%	4.30
Provides leadership to accelerate strategy implementation	45%	50%	5%	0%	0%	4.40
Engages and aligns key players	50%	50%	0%	0%	0%	4.50
Defines and implements detailed plans to execute the strategy	53%	26%	21%	0%	0%	4.32
Measures the impact of the sales strategy	45%	50%	0%	5%	0%	4.35

How important are the following key **knowledge areas** for effective performance?

Sales Strategy Definition and Execution: Key Knowledge	Critical (5)	Very important (4)	Moderately important (3)	Slightly important (2)	Not at all important (1)	Mean
Business profit/loss management methods	30%	45%	20%	5%	0%	4.00
Company business plans, market position, and strategic direction and goals	45%	45%	5%	5%	0%	4.30
Relationship between marketing efforts and initiatives and sales enablement	30%	45%	15%	10%	0%	3.95
Competitive knowledge and best practices	35%	30%	30%	5%	0%	3.95
Social media strategies and best practices	15%	40%	25%	10%	10%	3.40
Business standards of conduct and ethical business practices	35%	35%	20%	10%	0%	3.95
Cultural and market segment demographic shifts and diversity	35%	20%	35%	10%	0%	3.80
Ways to optimize online presence strategies, including social media for sales force and sales organization	26%	32%	32%	5%	5%	3.68
Executive relationship-building strategies	50%	40%	10%	0%	0%	4.40
Market dynamics (general and product/service-specific trends)	30%	50%	20%	0%	0%	4.10
Risk management and mitigation strategies	25%	35%	35%	5%	0%	3.80
Sales best practice and industry sales benchmarking resources	30%	30%	25%	10%	5%	3.70
Sales metrics, KPIs, and measurement methods	35%	50%	10%	0%	5%	4.10
Sales system/tool/process automation requirements	32%	26%	37%	0%	5%	3.79

How important are the following key **skills** for effective performance?

Sales Strategy Definition and Execution: Key Skills	Critical (5)	Very important (4)	Moderately important (3)	Slightly important (2)	Not at all important (1)	Mean
Respond to market challenges and opportunities systemically by developing actionable sales strategies	50%	40%	5%	5%	0%	4.35
Define sales force requirements based on analysis of industry/market dynamics	35%	45%	10%	10%	0%	4.05
Serve as a bridge between marketing and sales enablement by identifying sales activities that support marketing efforts and initiatives	40%	40%	15%	5%	0%	4.15
Share customer feedback about products and services with the company	50%	30%	20%	0%	0%	4.30
Span boundaries to develop cross-product/service line strategies	25%	55%	20%	0%	0%	4.05
Build executive sponsorship at the highest levels of the company	60%	30%	5%	5%	0%	4.45
Identify areas of risk and develop appropriate contingency plans	35%	35%	30%	0%	0%	4.05
Identify and leverage best sales practices within the organization	45%	45%	5%	5%	0%	4.30
Manage complex change or transformation programs for executing the sales strategy	55%	25%	15%	5%	0%	4.30
Optimize online presence strategies, including social media for sales force and sales organization	11%	44%	17%	22%	6%	3.33

AOE 7: Sales Team Management

How important are the following key **actions** for effective performance?

Sales Team Management: Key Actions	Critical (5)	Very important (4)	Moderately important (3)	Slightly important (2)	Not at all important (1)	Mean
Aligns tactical sales activities to strategic sales plans	64%	21%	14%	0%	0%	4.50
Sets budget and controls costs that impact sales margins	14%	36%	50%	0%	0%	3.64
Aligns resources with opportunities	36%	43%	21%	0%	0%	4.21
Ensures accurate forecasting	14%	36%	36%	14%	0%	3.50
Hires, promotes, and terminates sales team members	57%	29%	14%	0%	0%	4.43
Aligns reward and recognition strategies to performance goals	29%	57%	14%	0%	0%	4.14
Manages variety of sales management activities in a balanced way	29%	64%	7%	0%	0%	4.21
Leads a global, multicultural sales force	29%	43%	14%	0%	14%	3.71

How important are the following key **knowledge areas** for effective performance?

Sales Team Management: Key Knowledge	Critical (5)	Very important (4)	Moderately important (3)	Slightly important (2)	Not at all important (1)	Mean
Business standards of conduct and ethical guidelines	64%	7%	29%	0%	0%	4.36
Company KPIs	50%	36%	0%	14%	0%	4.21
Sales targets	57%	21%	21%	0%	0%	4.36
Sales incentive and compensation plans	29%	29%	36%	7%	0%	3.79
CRM applications and their use	36%	21%	36%	7%	0%	3.86
Pipeline management methods/tools	36%	29%	36%	0%	0%	4.00
Performance management techniques	36%	29%	36%	0%	0%	4.00
Human resources policies and procedures	21%	29%	29%	21%	0%	3.50
Organizational and operational processes	21%	43%	29%	7%	0%	3.79
Management processes and tools	29%	29%	29%	14%	0%	3.71
Margin management techniques	29%	21%	29%	21%	0%	3.57
Supply chain/order fulfillment processes/procedures	7%	7%	57%	21%	7%	2.86
SharePoint and repositories of sales collateral, tools, templates, etc.	0%	14%	50%	29%	7%	2.71
Available resources and approaches for sales talent development at individual and group level	14%	43%	36%	7%	0%	3.64
Sales force motivating and demotivating factors	50%	43%	7%	0%	0%	4.43

How important are the following key **skills** for effective performance?

Sales Team Management: Key Skills	Critical (5)	Very important (4)	Moderately important (3)	Slightly important (2)	Not at all important (1)	Mean
Apply approved methods to personnel management (hiring, terminating, promoting)	43%	36%	14%	0%	7%	4.07
Apply best practices in motivating employees and enhancing their morale and performance	38%	46%	8%	8%	0%	4.15
Assess individual or team strengths and weaknesses	50%	43%	7%	0%	0%	4.43
Build strategies for counteracting competitive tactics	21%	36%	36%	7%	0%	3.71
Ensure compliance to company policies and applicable local, national, and international laws and regulations	29%	36%	21%	14%	0%	3.79
Ensure sales force compliance to standards of conduct and ethical guidelines	43%	43%	7%	7%	0%	4.21
Identify and address sales force gaps (e.g., training, hiring)	43%	50%	7%	0%	0%	4.36
Build a succession or short-term replacement plan to deal with staff turnover and workload redistribution	21%	57%	21%	0%	0%	4.00
Manage business forecasts to ensure accuracy	14%	43%	36%	7%	0%	3.64
Manage operations to minimize costs or maximize profits	21%	57%	14%	7%	0%	3.93
Lead global, multicultural sales team	29%	36%	14%	7%	14%	3.57
Engage sales teams	43%	57%	0%	0%	0%	4.43
Maintain a talent pipeline	15%	38%	46%	0%	0%	3.69

AOE 8: Sales Coaching

How important are the following key **actions** for effective performance?

Sales Coaching: Key Actions	Critical (5)	Very important (4)	Moderately important (3)	Slightly important (2)	Not at all important (1)	Mean
Creates a climate that facilitates sales coaching	59%	31%	7%	3%	1%	4.43
Observes sales performance to identify opportunities for improvement	47%	37%	11%	0%	6%	4.19
Balances corrective feedback with positive feedback to improve performance	49%	38%	10%	3%	0%	4.34
Leverages motivation and reward as a key enabler of sales performance	36%	39%	15%	6%	4%	3.97
Connects performance expectations to strategic outcomes	46%	34%	12%	3%	6%	4.12
Models expected sales behaviors	51%	24%	13%	6%	7%	4.07
Approaches coaching as a continuous process	70%	23%	5%	1%	1%	4.60
Focuses on both results and behaviors	66%	25%	5%	2%	2%	4.52

How important are the following key **knowledge areas** for effective performance?

Sales Coaching: Key Knowledge	Critical (5)	Very important (4)	Moderately important (3)	Slightly important (2)	Not at all important (1)	Mean
Coaching methodology and techniques (both face-to-face and virtually)	55%	35%	8%	2%	0%	4.43
Listening and feedback delivery methods	65%	26%	6%	2%	1%	4.52
Performance critique and debriefing methods	53%	29%	13%	0%	5%	4.25
Performance observation techniques	51%	35%	10%	1%	3%	4.30
Performance review instruments and methods	36%	39%	19%	2%	4%	4.02
Sales excellence practices	51%	32%	14%	2%	1%	4.30
Generational workforce attributes and characteristics	25%	40%	26%	6%	2%	3.81

How important are the following key **skills** for effective performance?

Sales Coaching: Key Skills	Critical (5)	Very important (4)	Moderately important (3)	Slightly important (2)	Not at all important (1)	Mean
Assess performance objectively	61%	29%	6%	0%	4%	4.44
Determine areas for improvement (skills, knowledge, or performance) for individual sales team members	68%	28%	1%	1%	2%	4.59
Use a variety of questioning and listening techniques to facilitate self-discovery, learning, motivation, and performance improvement	56%	34%	7%	3%	0%	4.44
Build trust with sales team members through connection, competence, and communication	69%	21%	6%	2%	2%	4.53
Provide balanced (both positive and constructive) feedback	54%	33%	11%	1%	1%	4.39
Assume various roles as needed in role plays to maximize learning (e.g., sales person, customer, sales manager, technical support)	43%	38%	16%	3%	1%	4.18
Balance performance improvement objectives with a recipient's need for a healthy self-concept	41%	38%	17%	2%	2%	4.14
Employ observation to gather the most accurate performance data	49%	35%	14%	2%	1%	4.28
Identify "teachable moments" and use them to improve performance	57%	31%	10%	2%	0%	4.44
Focus on both the "how" and "what" of performance improvement	58%	27%	14%	0%	1%	4.42

AOE 9: Sales Talent Selection

How important are the following key **actions** for effective performance?

Sales Talent Selection: Key Actions	Critical (5)	Very important (4)	Moderately important (3)	Slightly important (2)	Not at all important (1)	Mean
Develops a solid understanding of the sales organization and sales culture	20%	80%	0%	0%	0%	4.20
Develops sales position descriptions	20%	60%	20%	0%	0%	4.00
Uses a disciplined, systematic, Equal Employment Opportunity Commission (EEOC)-compliant process to select sales professionals	0%	80%	20%	0%	0%	3.80
Aligns and modifies sales job profiles	0%	100%	0%	0%	0%	4.00
Ensures valid compensation packages	20%	40%	40%	0%	0%	3.80
Communicates with sales managers to adjust recruitment goals and job descriptions	0%	80%	20%	0%	0%	3.80
Monitors and maintains sales candidate pipeline	20%	80%	0%	0%	0%	4.20
Contacts, screens, and profiles candidates	0%	80%	20%	0%	0%	3.80
Generates offers and conducts negotiations with sales stakeholders to closure	20%	40%	40%	0%	0%	3.80
Supports orientation and onboarding	40%	20%	40%	0%	0%	4.00

How important are the following key **knowledge areas** for effective performance?

Sales Talent Selection: Key Knowledge	Critical (5)	Very important (4)	Moderately important (3)	Slightly important (2)	Not at all important (1)	Mean
EEOC laws, regulations, and policy guidance	20%	60%	20%	0%	0%	4.00
Requirements of the sales position (e.g., prior experience, company's strategy and type of sale, desired knowledge and attributes)	40%	60%	0%	0%	0%	4.40
Candidate pipeline management tools	0%	60%	40%	0%	0%	3.60
Company mission, vision, goals, and business strategy	60%	40%	0%	0%	0%	4.60
Linkage between marketing initiatives and sales activities	60%	0%	20%	20%	0%	4.00
Human resources recruitment policies, compliance requirements, and procedures	20%	40%	40%	0%	0%	3.80
Recruitment best practices	20%	60%	20%	0%	0%	4.00
How to read and interpret sales candidate assessments	20%	40%	20%	20%	0%	3.60
Interviewing methods and strategies (behavioral-based, probing techniques)	0%	60%	40%	0%	0%	3.60
Local, regional, country-level labor laws	20%	20%	60%	0%	0%	3.60
Negotiation methods	0%	60%	40%	0%	0%	3.60
Sales organization or company compensation structure and practices	0%	60%	40%	0%	0%	3.60
Sales or organizational culture and unique requirements	40%	20%	40%	0%	0%	4.00
Employee orientation, education, training and onboarding	40%	40%	20%	0%	0%	4.20
Succession planning	20%	20%	40%	20%	0%	3.40

How important are the following key **skills** for effective performance?

Sales Talent Selection: Key Skills	Critical (5)	Very important (4)	Moderately important (3)	Slightly important (2)	Not at all important (1)	Mean
Build and maintain contacts with colleges and professional recruitment agencies	0%	60%	40%	0%	0%	3.60
Use social media (i.e., LinkedIn, Facebook, Twitter, etc.) to identify and screen candidates	0%	80%	20%	0%	0%	3.80
Use understanding of the requirements of the position to identify, screen, and recruit qualified candidates	40%	60%	0%	0%	0%	4.40
Establish candidate relationships based on trust	0%	80%	20%	0%	0%	3.80
Influence the definition of job and salary requirements to ensure logical alignment	0%	100%	0%	0%	0%	4.00
Validate tacit impressions of a candidate through questioning techniques	0%	60%	20%	20%	0%	3.40
Protect the interests of company stakeholders during negotiations	0%	60%	40%	0%	0%	3.60
Facilitate new hire transition and integration within the sales organization	40%	40%	20%	0%	0%	4.20

AOE 10: Sales Talent Development

How important are the following key **actions** for effective performance?

Sales Talent Development: Key Actions	Critical (5)	Very important (4)	Moderately important (3)	Slightly important (2)	Not at all important (1)	Mean
Identifies competencies required to achieve the sales strategy	52%	30%	11%	5%	2%	4.26
Conducts sales-learning needs assessments	52%	28%	15%	4%	1%	4.27
Designs and develops sales talent development solutions	58%	25%	15%	2%	0%	4.40
Delivers learning solutions	68%	22%	8%	2%	0%	4.56
Implements and manages deployment of learning programs	68%	20%	10%	2%	0%	4.54
Creates sales onboarding programs	53%	27%	12%	3%	5%	4.21
Engages, drives, and manages sales audiences	38%	29%	20%	9%	4%	3.89
Evaluates sales learning effectiveness and impact	54%	31%	12%	3%	0%	4.37
Assesses sales competency	48%	32%	12%	6%	3%	4.16

How important are the following key **knowledge areas** for effective performance?

Sales Talent Development: Key Knowledge	Critical (5)	Very important (4)	Moderately important (3)	Slightly important (2)	Not at all important (1)	Mean
Learning style and preferences (i.e., individual, cultural, and generational)	48%	35%	15%	1%	1%	4.28
Adult learning principles and practices	60%	33%	6%	1%	1%	4.49
Training needs analysis	60%	30%	9%	1%	1%	4.46
Curriculum and learning road map design	58%	30%	8%	4%	1%	4.39
Blended learning strategies	51%	33%	13%	2%	1%	4.31
Experiential learning methods (e.g., work-based learning and on-the-job development techniques—mentoring, job rotation, job shadowing, case studies)	58%	31%	9%	2%	1%	4.42
Human performance improvement (HPI) principles and practices	33%	36%	24%	6%	1%	3.94
Innovative learning methods (e.g., mobile learning, gamification, blended learning, massive open online course [MOOC]) and when to use each to optimize learning	35%	35%	22%	7%	1%	3.96
Sales onboarding best practices	47%	30%	16%	5%	3%	4.13
Learning management systems (LMS)	31%	26%	32%	11%	1%	3.75
Customer relationship management (CRM)	25%	22%	34%	14%	5%	3.50
Learning program evaluation methods (formative and summative)	36%	43%	14%	5%	3%	4.04
Learning program ROI calculation methods	29%	38%	20%	9%	4%	3.80
Test development (item construction/validation)	28%	30%	28%	8%	6%	3.67
Sales competency assessment	46%	33%	12%	6%	3%	4.14

How important are the following key **skills** for effective performance?

Sales Talent Development: Key Skills	Critical (5)	Very important (4)	Moderately important (3)	Slightly important (2)	Not at all important (1)	Mean
Translate business requirements into requirements for learning and development solutions	64%	24%	11%	1%	0%	4.52
Conduct learning and development needs analysis	60%	27%	13%	1%	0%	4.45
Review and assess individual and role-based learning and development plans	44%	33%	17%	6%	0%	4.15
Obtain stakeholders' approval and buy-in on strategic talent development plans and required learning investment	49%	33%	13%	5%	1%	4.24
Apply effective delivery and facilitation methods to engage learners and to advance learning	63%	30%	6%	1%	0%	4.56
Apply rapid instructional design methods to ensure timely development of learning solutions	40%	34%	20%	4%	2%	4.07
Build learning solutions responsive to learner characteristics (e.g., learning styles, generational demographics, availability, technical readiness, cultural norms)	42%	36%	16%	3%	3%	4.12
Use workplace opportunities to create experiential learning solutions (e.g., mentoring, coaching, peer-to-peer tutoring, case studies)	49%	37%	10%	3%	2%	4.28
Build valid and reliable tests to measure learning	37%	38%	18%	6%	1%	4.04
Select the most appropriate learning approach based on factors such as cost, urgency, and target audience requirements	44%	34%	19%	3%	0%	4.19
Implement learning program evaluation systematically to measure the effectiveness and business impact of learning solutions	43%	36%	12%	9%	1%	4.11
Leverage learning technologies and platforms to optimize learning	46%	26%	22%	4%	2%	4.11

AOE 11: Sales Tool and Process Improvement

How important are the following key **actions** for effective performance?

Sales Tool and Process Improvement: Key Actions	Critical (5)	Very important (4)	Moderately important (3)	Slightly important (2)	Not at all important (1)	Mean
Monitors current sales tools and processes for improvement opportunities	23%	38%	38%	0%	0%	3.85
Develops and drives process/tool planning	15%	38%	38%	8%	0%	3.62
Educates sales teams on KPIs, processes, and systems	31%	23%	38%	0%	8%	3.69
Creates data and information feed to stakeholders	23%	38%	23%	8%	8%	3.62
Manages process/tool upkeep or revision	31%	15%	23%	23%	8%	3.38
Drives or supports sales process/tool change and alignment	31%	23%	31%	8%	8%	3.62
Evaluates impact of process/tool change programs	31%	31%	31%	8%	0%	3.85

How important are the following key **knowledge areas** for effective performance?

Sales Tool and Process Improvement: Key Knowledge	Critical (5)	Very important (4)	Moderately important (3)	Slightly important (2)	Not at all important (1)	Mean
Change management methodologies	23%	38%	38%	0%	0%	3.85
Company's sales process, its phases, requirements, and tools	46%	31%	23%	0%	0%	4.23
CRM systems and the benefits of aligning the sales pipeline component of the CRM to sales process	38%	31%	8%	8%	15%	3.69
Data mining and analysis methods and technology	31%	8%	46%	0%	15%	3.38
Innovative learning delivery systems/media (e-learning, mobile learning, gamification, MOOC, and digital sales playbooks)	23%	46%	23%	8%	0%	3.85
Innovative sales operations productivity tools and technologies (CRM, social media, and mobile applications)	23%	46%	23%	8%	0%	3.85
Quality management tools and processes	23%	31%	31%	8%	8%	3.54
Process analysis and planning methods	31%	23%	31%	0%	15%	3.54
Stakeholders' requirements definition and tracking methods	31%	31%	23%	8%	8%	3.69
ROI calculation methods and tools	23%	54%	15%	0%	8%	3.85
KPIs that provide insight into sales force effectiveness using leading and lagging indicators	23%	31%	38%	0%	8%	3.62
Sales operations functions and processes	38%	23%	31%	0%	8%	3.85
Performance support systems, tools, and job aids	38%	31%	15%	15%	0%	3.92

How important are the following key **skills** for effective performance?

Sales Tool and Process Improvement: Key Skills	Critical (5)	Very important (4)	Moderately important (3)	Slightly important (2)	Not at all important (1)	Mean
Conduct current and future state gap assessment to define requirements for improving sales tools and processes	38%	31%	23%	8%	0%	4.00
Educate sales professionals on KPIs, sales process, and benefits of sales process; train sales managers on coaching sales process adherence	38%	31%	23%	0%	8%	3.92
Build models depicting all stakeholder interfaces to common tools and applications	38%	23%	15%	8%	15%	3.62
Define requirements for and provide needed data and intelligence to all key stakeholders	23%	31%	38%	0%	8%	3.62
Manage or support the planning and implementation of innovations	31%	31%	38%	0%	0%	3.92
Monitor and assess the value of emerging tools and processes to improve sales productivity and enablement	23%	54%	15%	0%	8%	3.85
Identify, select, and manage tools and process improvement vendors	15%	38%	23%	15%	8%	3.38
Use the sales pipeline data to identify opportunities for sales process improvement and work with stakeholders to develop a plan of action to improve performance	15%	54%	15%	0%	15%	3.54

AOE 12: Sales Incentive and Compensation Design

How important are the following key **actions** for effective performance?

Incentive and Compensation Design: Key Actions	Critical (5)	Very important (4)	Moderately important (3)	Slightly important (2)	Not at all important (1)	Mean
Assesses current compensation and incentive programs against best practices	0%	100%	0%	0%	0%	4.00
Aligns compensation and incentive campaigns with business requirements and appropriate sales behaviors and metrics	100%	0%	0%	0%	0%	5.00
Obtains support for sales compensation plans	0%	100%	0%	0%	0%	4.00
Drives organizational acceptance of sales compensation changes	0%	0%	100%	0%	0%	3.00
Measures business impact of incentive programs	0%	100%	0%	0%	0%	4.00

How important are the following key **knowledge areas** for effective performance?

Incentive and Compensation Design: Key Knowledge	Critical (5)	Very important (4)	Moderately important (3)	Slightly important (2)	Not at all important (1)	Mean
Compensation research and benchmark sources	0%	0%	0%	100%	0%	2.00
Financial compensation and incentive methods and metrics	0%	0%	100%	0%	0%	3.00
Industry compensation and incentive practices and standards	0%	0%	100%	0%	0%	3.00
Local, regional, and/or country-level regulatory requirements	0%	0%	0%	100%	0%	2.00
Payout processes, key milestones, ratios, and formulas	0%	0%	100%	0%	0%	3.00
Program planning and management skills	0%	0%	100%	0%	0%	3.00
Sales force motivators	100%	0%	0%	0%	0%	5.00
Methods and approaches to measure the business impact of incentive and compensation programs	0%	100%	0%	0%	0%	4.00

How important are the following key **skills** for effective performance?

Incentive and Compensation Design: Key Skills	Critical (5)	Very important (4)	Moderately important (3)	Slightly important (2)	Not at all important (1)	Mean
Build business cases and generate stakeholder buy-in for incentive and compensation programs	0%	0%	100%	0%	0%	3.00
Determine competitive yet feasible compensation metrics	0%	100%	0%	0%	0%	4.00
Create compelling but flexible and nimble compensation programs proportionate to degree of transformation and change desired	100%	0%	0%	0%	0%	5.00
Identify and incorporate market competitive practices into compensation and incentive campaigns	0%	100%	0%	0%	0%	4.00
Identify the impact of current and proposed compensation policies on company health and sales force retention or recruiting	0%	100%	0%	0%	0%	4.00
Manage compensation change programs	0%	100%	0%	0%	0%	4.00
Supplement base payout with innovative reward and recognition strategies	0%	100%	0%	0%	0%	4.00
Select, engage, and manage partners and vendors to implement reward and incentive programs (e.g., goods and services for incentive campaigns and travel and venues for reward programs)	0%	0%	100%	0%	0%	3.00
Use software applications for implementing compensation plans	0%	0%	0%	100%	0%	2.00

Part 3: Sales Foundational Competencies Validation

In this section we asked respondents to rate the importance of *Key Actions* in four clusters of foundational competencies that are critical to their success, using the following 5-point scale.

   5—**Critical** (It is crucial to my success)
   4—**Very Important** (It is important)
   3—**Moderately Important** (It has a moderate level of importance)
   2—**Slightly Important** (It has some importance to my success)
   1—**Not at all important** (It has little or no importance to my success).

These are the four foundational competency clusters:
- Collaboration Competencies
- Insight Competencies
- Solution Competencies
- Effectiveness Competencies.

Collaboration Competencies

How important for effective performance are each of the following key **actions** in the *Collaboration Competencies* cluster?

Relationship Building	Critical (5)	Very important (4)	Moderately important (3)	Slightly important (2)	Not at all important (1)	Mean
Actively nurtures positive relationships	58.7%	36.8%	3.1%	0.7%	0.7%	4.5
Develops and leverages relationships to achieve results	52.8%	40.6%	4.9%	1.0%	0.7%	4.4
Protects the integrity of relationships	60.3%	33.8%	4.2%	1.0%	0.7%	4.5

Alignment Building	Critical (5)	Very important (4)	Moderately important (3)	Slightly important (2)	Not at all important (1)	Mean
Positions work meaningfully in terms of its relationship to other functions	30.4%	54.3%	12.8%	1.7%	0.7%	4.1
Advocates collaboration and establishes positive relationships across organizational boundaries	40.5%	45.3%	10.7%	2.4%	1.0%	4.2
Serves as a role model within the company	40.1%	41.5%	16.3%	1.4%	0.7%	4.2
Recognizes and addresses gaps between personal, team, or organizational responsibilities	33.6%	48.1%	12.5%	4.5%	1.4%	4.1

Strategic Partnering	Critical (5)	Very important (4)	Moderately important (3)	Slightly important (2)	Not at all important (1)	Mean
Maintains a solid understanding of customer challenges	52.4%	34.4%	11.1%	1.0%	1.0%	4.4
Understands the rationale behind strategies and initiatives and actively contributes to their successful implementation	40.6%	44.8%	12.5%	1.0%	1.0%	4.2
Continuously evaluates work in terms of its contribution to meeting business needs	39.9%	43.8%	13.8%	1.4%	1.1%	4.2

Teaming	Critical (5)	Very important (4)	Moderately important (3)	Slightly important (2)	Not at all important (1)	Mean
Maintains understanding of effective team processes	27.3%	51.9%	16.3%	2.8%	1.7%	4.0
Proactively strives to maintain high team performance	35.4%	46.2%	13.5%	2.8%	2.1%	4.1
Capitalizes on the strengths of individual members to achieve team goals	41.3%	41.0%	12.5%	3.5%	1.7%	4.2
Operates effectively on virtual teams	23.1%	40.9%	21.0%	8.4%	6.6%	3.7

Transformational Leadership	Critical (5)	Very important (4)	Moderately important (3)	Slightly important (2)	Not at all important (1)	Mean
Drives change and innovation in a way that instills confidence in others	41.7%	38.9%	14.9%	3.8%	0.7%	4.2
Provides the mindset critical for implementing continuous improvement and transformation sensitively and effectively	39.2%	39.2%	17.8%	2.8%	1.0%	4.1

Customer Advocacy	Critical (5)	Very important (4)	Moderately important (3)	Slightly important (2)	Not at all important (1)	Mean
Ensures customer satisfaction	64.0%	27.0%	5.9%	2.4%	0.7%	4.5
Advocates for the customer	49.5%	35.5%	10.8%	3.5%	0.7%	4.3

Insight Competencies

How important for effective performance are each of the following key **actions** in the *Insight Competencies* cluster?

Business and Financial Acumen	Critical (5)	Very important (4)	Moderately important (3)	Slightly important (2)	Not at all important (1)	Mean
Understands what it takes to manage a business	33.9%	39.8%	17.6%	6.9%	1.7%	4.0
Applies business insight in opportunity analysis	31.9%	41.3%	19.4%	4.2%	3.1%	4.0
Positions the financial benefits associated with proposed solution	32.2%	43.4%	16.4%	5.9%	2.1%	4.0

Sector/Industry Insight	Critical (5)	Very important (4)	Moderately important (3)	Slightly important (2)	Not at all important (1)	Mean
Builds reliable sector/industry networks and resources	28.2%	47.7%	17.1%	4.2%	2.8%	3.9
Actively monitors the sector/industry landscape for emerging challenges and changes	26.7%	45.3%	21.4%	4.6%	2.1%	3.9

Evaluating Customer Experiences	Critical (5)	Very important (4)	Moderately important (3)	Slightly important (2)	Not at all important (1)	Mean
Evaluates the effectiveness and business impact of solutions	38.5%	42.7%	3.8%	42.7%	0.7%	4.1
Communicates results in terms of bottom-line business metrics to stakeholders	39.6%	35.1%	3.9%	35.1%	3.5%	4.0

Research/Analysis	Critical (5)	Very important (4)	Moderately important (3)	Slightly important (2)	Not at all important (1)	Mean
Determines the range, type, and scope of information needed	27.5%	45.6%	22.0%	2.4%	2.4%	3.9
Applies the most appropriate tools and strategies to gather needed information	24.0%	51.6%	18.8%	3.1%	2.4%	3.9
Incorporates information effectively into action	40.2%	41.3%	14.3%	1.7%	2.4%	4.2

Solution Competencies

How important for effective performance are each of the following key **actions** in the *Solution Competencies* cluster?

Product/Service Acumen	Critical (5)	Very important (4)	Moderately important (3)	Slightly important (2)	Not at all important (1)	Mean
Maintains a solid understanding of product/ service offerings	51.9%	37.7%	8.0%	1.7%	0.7%	4.4
Understands solution components and how they add value	53.5%	35.3%	8.4%	1.7%	1.0%	4.4

Competitive Intelligence	Critical (5)	Very important (4)	Moderately important (3)	Slightly important (2)	Not at all important (1)	Mean
Stays current with the competitive landscape	33.0%	45.5%	15.6%	3.8%	2.1%	4.0
Ensures that competitor claims are appropriately vetted in solution definition and planning	21.3%	41.6%	22.0%	8.7%	6.3%	3.6
Understands competitor's strategies and tactics	26.6%	37.1%	24.5%	8.0%	3.8%	3.8

Consultative Insight	Critical (5)	Very important (4)	Moderately important (3)	Slightly important (2)	Not at all important (1)	Mean
Challenges the customer by providing a wider perspective to solution definition	35.8%	39.9%	17.4%	4.2%	2.8%	4.0
Ensures that solutions are justified and in the best interest of the customer	44.8%	39.9%	9.7%	3.8%	1.7%	4.2
Ensures that the proposed solutions satisfy customer needs	52.1%	35.1%	8.3%	2.8%	1.7%	4.3
Maintains involvement in online communities	11.3%	26.8%	33.5%	16.9%	11.6%	3.1

Negotiating and Gaining Commitment	Critical (5)	Very important (4)	Moderately important (3)	Slightly important (2)	Not at all important (1)	Mean
Effectively plans and prepares for negotiations	38.8%	33.2%	14.9%	5.2%	8.0%	3.9
Determines optimum bargaining position	27.4%	37.8%	19.4%	5.9%	9.4%	3.7
Builds value propositions	45.8%	32.3%	12.5%	4.5%	4.9%	4.1
Applies appropriate techniques to reach agreements	35.8%	36.1%	16.5%	5.3%	6.3%	3.9

Complex Problem Solving	Critical (5)	Very important (4)	Moderately important (3)	Slightly important (2)	Not at all important (1)	Mean
Approaches challenges creatively	43.9%	43.6%	10.4%	1.7%	0.3%	4.3
Crosses disciplines to frame or address challenges	36.2%	44.6%	15.7%	2.4%	1.0%	4.1

Effectiveness Competencies

How important for effective performance are each of the following key **actions** in the *Effectiveness Competencies* cluster?

Diversity Effectiveness	Critical (5)	Very important (4)	Moderately important (3)	Slightly important (2)	Not at all important (1)	Mean
Demonstrates respect for others	55.0%	35.6%	7.3%	1.7%	0.3%	4.4
Adapts to diverse work settings	43.9%	40.0%	12.6%	2.5%	1.1%	4.2
Harnesses diversity to create workplace synergies	32.2%	39.9%	22.0%	3.1%	2.8%	4.0

Global Awareness	Critical (5)	Very important (4)	Moderately important (3)	Slightly important (2)	Not at all important (1)	Mean
Incorporates a global perspective to accommodate others	18.1%	36.6%	25.1%	10.1%	10.1%	3.4
Ensures the effectiveness of global communications	16.7%	36.1%	23.6%	11.8%	11.8%	3.3
Adapts tactics to maintain the momentum of global initiatives	13.7%	35.9%	26.4%	12.0%	12.0%	3.3

Multigenerational Effectiveness	Critical (5)	Very important (4)	Moderately important (3)	Slightly important (2)	Not at all important (1)	Mean
Develops a solid understanding of generational differences as the basis for effective interaction	27.2%	40.3%	21.4%	8.3%	2.8%	3.8
Builds and incorporates the tactics critical for working effectively with generational differences	26.3%	39.1%	23.5%	8.3%	2.8%	3.8

Sales Process Acumen	Critical (5)	Very important (4)	Moderately important (3)	Slightly important (2)	Not at all important (1)	Mean
Maintains a solid understanding of sales methodology	38.4%	40.5%	14.2%	4.5%	2.4%	4.1
Aligns and relates work to sales process	35.8%	40.6%	14.9%	6.6%	2.1%	4.0

Technology Fluency	Critical (5)	Very important (4)	Moderately important (3)	Slightly important (2)	Not at all important (1)	Mean
Understands how technology supports optimum performance and seeks to master tool or system innovations	25.7%	48.6%	20.5%	3.8%	1.4%	3.9
Effectively incorporates technology into work	28.5%	47.2%	17.4%	5.2%	1.7%	4.0
Embraces personal productivity technology	22.9%	45.1%	25.7%	4.9%	1.4%	3.8

Project Management	Critical (5)	Very important (4)	Moderately important (3)	Slightly important (2)	Not at all important (1)	Mean
Organizes and manages work systematically	34.9%	52.6%	9.3%	2.1%	1.0%	4.2
Organizes and manages resources effectively	38.8%	50.9%	8.0%	1.7%	0.7%	4.3
Adaptively applies methods as needed to achieve goals	31.0%	56.6%	10.3%	1.8%	0.4%	4.2

Effective Communication	Critical (5)	Very important (4)	Moderately important (3)	Slightly important (2)	Not at all important (1)	Mean
Listens actively	76.2%	20.0%	3.4%	0.3%	0.0%	4.7
Achieves communication objectives	55.7%	37.0%	6.6%	0.0%	0.7%	4.5
Communicates persuasively	58.9%	37.6%	2.8%	0.3%	0.3%	4.5
Uses storytelling	42.9%	31.1%	20.1%	4.8%	1.0%	4.1

Ethical Decision Making	Critical (5)	Very important (4)	Moderately important (3)	Slightly important (2)	Not at all important (1)	Mean
Demonstrates personal integrity	77.6%	19.0%	3.1%	0.0%	0.3%	4.7
Incorporates quality considerations into decision making	59.7%	34.0%	5.2%	0.7%	0.3%	4.5

APPENDIX E

TOOLS FOR ORGANIZATIONS TO CONDUCT COMPETENCY ASSESSMENT

The new ATD World-Class Sales Competency Model (WCSCM), like any other competency model, is a means to an end, not an end in and of itself. It provides sales organizations with a state-of-the-art competency framework that can be a critical tool for achieving a variety of sales talent management goals.

To adapt the model to your organization's needs as well as your own, chapters 6 and 7, respectively, describe the steps to take. This appendix provides the following tools, templates, and examples for more effective use of the WCSCM in conducting competency gap assessments.

- Appendix E.1—Job Aid for Building Customized Self-Assessment Tools
  - E.1.1—Self-Assessment Tool: Template
- Appendix E.2—Setting Proficiency Targets for Competency Assessment: Template
- Appendix E.3—Aggregating and Finalizing Proficiency Targets: Template
- Appendix E.4—Competency Gap Assessment: Example
- Appendix E.5—Capturing and Reporting Capability and Capacity Analysis: Template

Appendix E.1—Job Aid for Building Customized Self-Assessment Tools

Overview

This job aid provides step-by-step instructions for using the ATD WCSCM to create customized self-assessment tools that meet the unique requirements of your organization. Key steps in the process are illustrated through developing a self-assessment tool for inside sales representatives (ISR) in a sales organization. Appendix E.1.1 contains the template for building self-assessment tools.

How Is a Self-Assessment Tool Used?

The self-assessment tool enables employees to assess their strengths and opportunities for development in order to create an individual plan. Using areas of expertise (AOEs) and foundational competencies in the WCSCM to prepare assessment tools ensures accurate and objective assessment of sales force competency strengths and opportunities for competency development.

What You Need to Build a Customized Self-Assessment Tool

You will need the following two documents to create a self-assessment tool:

- Self-Assessment Tool Template—Provides the framework upon which you will build your self-assessment tool. You will need to customize the template for the role you select. The following is a brief description of the major sections of the template:
  - Title and Introduction—Identifies and describes the tool.
  - AOE Assessment Section—Includes items covering selected AOEs.
  - Foundational Competency Assessment Section—Includes items covering foundational competencies.
  - Self-Assessment Rating—Provides input areas to enter self-assessment ratings for AOEs and foundational competencies items.
- World-Class Sales Competency Model—Provides the AOEs and foundational competencies that you will use to customize the self-assessment tool for a specific role.

How to Build a Customized Self-Assessment Tool

Follow the steps described to build your customized self-assessment tool.

Step 1. Identify the Target Role and Customize the Title Information

You may create a self-assessment tool for any sales role covered by the WCSCM. In the title area, simply replace the text SALES ROLE with the selected role (for example, Inside Sales Representative).

Self-Assessment Tool:
INSIDE SALES REPRESENTATIVE

TIP: The following table identifies some sales roles that fall under each of the three parts of the WCSCM:

Sales Force	Sales Management and Leadership	Sales Enablement
• Sales representative • Account manager • Sales specialist • Presales consultant • Inside sale • Partner sale	• Sales manager • Sales director/ executive • Presales/Sales specialist manager	• Sales trainer • Sales coach • Sales recruiter • Sales operations • Sales compensation

Step 2. Identify AOEs and Foundational Competencies

Referring to the WCSCM, create a list of the AOEs and foundational competencies that you would like to include in the self-assessment for your selected role.

TIP: Determine the AOEs and foundational competencies to use for the self-assessment tool based on the strategic direction of the sales organization and the responsibilities of the specific role (for example, Inside Sales Representative or Sales Manager) you have selected.

TIP: You may want to customize the WCSCM to the sales role prior to creating your self-assessment.

Inside Sales Representative (ISR) Example—As part of a strategic initiative, a sales organization is redefining the role of Inside Sales Representative. This role is now expected to be engaged in the end-to-end sales cycle and to proactively identify, qualify, propose, and close opportunities. Based on these requirements, the most relevant AOEs for the new ISR role are included in the following table. You might also want to include all sales foundational competencies because they are core and common to all sales roles.

AOEs: 1. Account Development and Retention 5. Sales Pipeline and Forecast Management
Foundational Competencies: • Strategic Partnering • Customer Advocacy • Sales Process Acumen

Step 3. Expand the Template

Copy and paste the rows of the Self-Assessment Tool Template to provide space for all of the AOEs and foundational competencies, as shown. Insert rows for additional AOEs and foundational competencies that you would like to include in the self-assessment for your selected role.

	Self-Assessment Rating
AOE: Add AOE Title:	0.00
Assessment items:	
1.	
2.	
3.	
4.	
5.	
6.	
Foundational Competency:	0.00
Assessment items:	
1.	
2.	
3.	
4.	
5.	
6.	

Step 4. Enter the AOE Information

Referring to the WCSCM, copy and paste the following information for each AOE:

- Enter the title of the AOE on the first line.
- Enter on the numbered lines below the AOE the "Key Knowledge" and "Key Skills" from the WCSCM that are **relevant** and **critical** to the role in your organization.

TIP: Add, remove, or modify "Key Knowledge" and "Key Skill" items to tailor the self-assessment tool to the role being assessed and your organizational needs.

		Self-Assessment Rating
Area of Expertise: Account Development and Retention		0.00
Assessment items:		
1.	Knowledge of account farming procedures/practices (e.g., check-ins)	
2.	Knowledge of account history and contacts (i.e., prior investments, account relationships)	
3.	Knowledge of account planning tool and templates	
4.	Foundational knowledge of business metrics (e.g., health ratios, return on investment [ROI], total cost of ownership)	
5.	Knowledge of competitive information resources	
6.	Knowledge of contract administration and renewal processes and resources	
7.	Knowledge of back-office administrative/order-entry procedures	
8.	Knowledge of product/service features, benefits, and value propositions	
9.	Ability to manage leads and referrals	
10.	Ability to coordinate and align account activities with the account plan	
11.	Ability to apply pipeline management practices, tools, metrics, and policies to prioritize and manage selling	
12.	Ability to leverage contract administration and renewal into opportunities for up- and cross-selling	
13.	Ability to manage total customer satisfaction to optimize relationships	
14.	Ability to set accurate customer expectations for order fulfillment (e.g., lead times, response rates, fulfillment processes)	
15.	Ability to translate competitive knowledge into relevant competitive countering messages	

Step 5. Enter the Foundational Competency Information

Referring to the WCSCM, copy and paste the following information for each foundational competency cluster:

- Enter the title and description of the foundational competency on the first line.
- Enter on the numbered lines below the foundational competency the "Key Actions" from the WCSCM that are relevant and critical to the role in your organization.

TIP: Add, remove, or modify "Key Actions" items to tailor the self-assessment tool to the role being assessed and your organizational needs.

Cluster 4: Professional Effectiveness Competencies—Demonstrate the following competencies: • Strategic Partnering • Customer Advocacy • Sales Process Acumen	
Assessment Items:	
Strategic Partnering	
Maintains a solid understanding of customer challenges	
Understands the rationale behind strategies and initiatives and actively contributes to their successful implementation	
Continuously evaluates work in terms of its contribution to meeting business needs	
Customer Advocacy	
Ensures customer satisfaction	
Advocates for the customer	
Sales Process Acumen	
Maintains a solid understanding of sales methodology	
Aligns and relates work to sales process	

Appendix E.1.1—Self-Assessment Tool: Template

Title: Identifies and describes the tool

Self-Assessment Tool: SALES ROLE
Read each item carefully and provide a rating using the following 5-point scale: 1— Strong Development Need 2—Development Need 3—Opportunity for Growth 4—Solid 5—Strength to Leverage NA—Not Applicable.

Competency Assessment Section: Includes items covering selected AOEs

	Self-Assessment Rating
AOE 1: New Account Acquisition:	0.00
Assessment items:	
1.	
2.	
3.	
4.	
5.	
6.	
Foundational Competency:	0.00
Assessment items:	
1.	
2.	
3.	
4.	
5.	
6.	

Appendix E.2—Setting Proficiency Targets for Competency Assessment: Template

Use the following template to determine which AOEs and foundational competencies are most important to the success of the organization. This is a critical task and will help determine the desired proficiency level to be used as criteria for determining competency gaps. The information will also be used for sales capability and capacity planning.

	Template for Setting Proficiency Targets for AOE 1 (New Account Acquisition)	
	Note: If needed, replace these items with the items that you customized, using the instructions described in Appendix E.1	

Instructions

Using your knowledge of the organization's strategic business direction, as well as your own personal experiences, for EACH item, please determine how critical this item is to the success of the business, using a 5-point scale:

5—Very Critical
4—Critical
3—Important
2—Somewhat Important
1—Less Important

Save the file and return it to XXXX@XXX.com.

Item #	AOE 1: New Account Acquisition	Rating
Key Knowledge—Successful performance requires knowledge of:		
1.	Product/service features, drawbacks, benefits, and value propositions	
2.	Prospect business and financial health information, including key performance indicators (KPIs)	
3.	Resource knowledge (e.g., marketing/industry, technical, pricing, legal, delivery, and fulfillment)	
4.	Lead generation and management procedures	
5.	Hunting and opportunity discovery techniques and best practices	
6.	Objection and drawbacks handling techniques	
7.	Competitive analysis and positioning resources	
8.	Opportunity qualification and sizing techniques	
9.	Sales cycle management techniques	
10.	Social media sites and connectivity applications	
11.	Company's selling process (including sales process phases, phase definitions and the requirements to advance an opportunity from one phase)	
12.	Company's core competencies	
13.	Company's pricing guidelines, including discount and approval process	
14.	Customer relationship management (CRM) best practices	
15.	Buyers' business challenges and their drivers	
16.	Business standards of conduct and ethical business practices	

Item #	AOE 1: New Account Acquisition	Rating
Key Skills—Successful performance requires the ability to:		
1.	Define engagement strategies based on assessment of a prospect and likelihood to buy	
2.	Adjust engagement tactics based on a careful reading of a prospect's receptiveness	
3.	Execute hunting and opportunity discovery efforts with persistence in the face of rejection	
4.	Engage prospects in an exploratory conversation about their needs by focusing on listening, analyzing the information, summarizing their needs to confirm understanding, and avoiding a direct sales pitch	
5.	Leverage market and industry insights accurately when positioning offers	
6.	Manage leads and ensure follow-up/follow-through	
7.	Map prospect management structure and decision-making authority	
8.	Track and manage multiple sales opportunities and prospect engagements	
9.	Identify the prospect's purchase drivers (e.g., their needs, priorities, problems to be solved, or opportunities to be realized)	
10.	Adapt and deliver sales presentations that speak to the prospect's most urgent needs	
11.	Follow the sales process and utilize integrated customer relationship management (CRM) systems to manage and advance opportunities to closure and provide complete, accurate, and timely information	
12.	Pursue global sales opportunities with sensitivity to cultural differences	
13.	Present value propositions in compelling stories	
14.	Identify issues that might require a need to modify the sales approach	

Appendix E.3—Aggregating and Finalizing Proficiency Targets: Template

Use the following template to collect proficiency targets from individual leaders, to aggregate their input, to set a single proficiency target for each item, and to obtain approval from business sponsors. Note: Use additional columns, depending on the number of leaders providing proficiency targets.

AOE 1: New Account Acquisition		Proficiency Target Average	Leader 1	Leader 2	Leader 3	Leader n
1.	Product/service features, drawbacks, benefits, and value propositions	4.25	4.00	5.00	4.00	4.00
2.	Prospect business and financial health information, including key performance indicators (KPIs)					
3.	Resource knowledge (e.g., marketing/industry, technical, pricing, legal, delivery, and fulfillment)					
4.	Lead generation and management procedures					
5.	Hunting and opportunity discovery techniques and best practices					
6.	Objection and drawbacks handling techniques					
7.	Competitive analysis and positioning resources					
8.	Opportunity qualification and sizing techniques					
9.	Sales cycle management techniques					
10.	Social media sites and connectivity applications					
11.	Company's selling process (including sales process phases, phase definitions and the requirements to advance an opportunity from one phase)					
12.	Company's core competencies					
13.	Company's pricing guidelines including discount and approval process					
14.	Customer relationship management (CRM) best practices					
15.	Buyers' business challenges and their drivers					
16.	Business standards of conduct and ethical business practices					
17.	Define engagement strategies based on assessment of a prospect and their likelihood to buy					
18.	Adjust engagement tactics based on a careful reading of a prospect's receptiveness					
19.	Execute hunting and opportunity discovery efforts with persistence in the face of rejection					

AOE 1: New Account Acquisition (continued)		Proficiency Target Average	Leader 1	Leader 2	Leader 3	Leader n
20.	Engage prospects in an exploratory conversation about their needs by focusing on listening, analyzing the information, summarizing their needs to confirm understanding, and avoiding a direct sales pitch					
21.	Leverage market and industry insights accurately when positioning offers					
22.	Manage leads and ensure follow-up/follow-through					
23.	Map prospect management structure and decision-making authority					
24.	Track and manage multiple sales opportunities and prospect engagements					
25.	Identify the prospect's purchase drivers (e.g., their needs, priorities, problems to be solved, or opportunities to be realized)					
26.	Adapt and deliver sales presentations that speak to the prospect's most urgent needs					
27.	Follow the sales process and utilize integrated customer relationship management (CRM) systems to manage and advance opportunities to closure and provide complete, accurate, and timely information					
28.	Pursue global sales opportunities with sensitivity to cultural differences					
29.	Present value propositions in compelling stories					
30.	Identify issues that might require a need to modify the sales approach					

Appendix E.4—Competency Gap Assessment Example

Personal Assessment Report—First Name Last Name
Average Ratings for AEOs and Foundational Competencies: Target and Self-Ratings

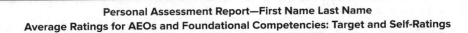

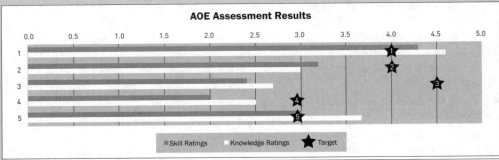

AOE Assessment Results

Legend: Skill Ratings | Knowledge Ratings | ★ Target

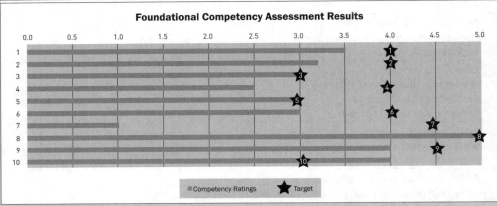

Foundational Competency Assessment Results

Legend: Competency Ratings | ★ Target

Areas of Expertise (AOE)	Targets	Skill Ratings	Knowledge Ratings
1. New Account Acquistion	4.0	4.3	4.6
2. Account Development and Retention	4.0	3.2	3.0
3. Complex Solution Definition and Positioning	4.5	2.4	2.7
4. Partner Sales Support	3.0	2.0	2.5
5. Sales Pipeline and Forecast Management	3.0	3.0	3.7

Solid Strength = -2.1 or less	
Strength = -1.1 to -2.0	
Within Range = -1.0 to +1.0	
Development Need = +1.1 to +2.0	
Strong Development Need = +2.1 or above	

Foundational Competencies	Target	Competency Rating
1. Relationship Building	4.0	3.5
2. Teaming	4.0	3.2
3. Business and Financial Acumen	3.0	3.0
4. Sector/Industry Insight	4.0	2.5
5. Product Services Acumen	3.0	3.0
6. Negotiating and Gaining Commitment	4.0	3.0
7. Competitive Intelligence	4.5	1.0
8. Ethical Decision Making	5.0	5.0
9. Effective Communication & Presentation	4.5	4.0
10. Sales Process Acumen	3.0	4.0

Appendix E.5—Capturing and Reporting Capability and Capacity Analysis: Template

Instructions:

- Add select AOE titles and foundational competency titles to the first column.
- Place a check mark in the Critical Capabilities column for competencies rated 4 or 5.
- Add titles to Current Capacity columns (for example, geographies, business units).
- Add percentage of participants who provided a rating of 4 or 5 for these AOEs and foundational competencies.

Areas of Expertise (AOE) and Foundational Competencies	Critical Capabilities	Current Capacity			
		Enterprise	Geo/BU 1	Geo/BU 2	Geo/BU 3
Areas of Expertise (AOE)					
AOE Title	✓	—	—	—	—
AOE Title					
AOE Title					
AOE Title					
AOE Title					
AOE Title					
AOE Title					
AOE Title					
Foundational Competencies					
Cluster 1: Collaboration					
Foundational Competency Title					
Foundational Competency Title					
Foundational Competency Title					
Foundational Competency Title					
Cluster 2: Insight					
Foundational Competency Title					
Foundational Competency Title					
Foundational Competency Title					
Foundational Competency Title					
Cluster 3: Solution					
Foundational Competency Title					

(continued)

Appendix E.5—Capturing and Reporting Capability and Capacity Analysis: Template (continued)

Foundational Competency Title					
Foundational Competency Title					
Cluster 4: Effectiveness					
Foundational Competency Title					
Foundational Competency Title					
Foundational Competency Title					
Foundational Competency Title					
Foundational Competency Title					
Foundational Competency Title					

APPENDIX F

TOOLS FOR ORGANIZATIONS TO BUILD HIRING GUIDES

This appendix introduces hiring guides as a tool to be used for screening and selecting sales job candidates. It provides step-by-step instructions for creating hiring guides utilizing the ATD World-Class Sales Competency Model (WCSCM). Key steps in the process are illustrated through developing a hiring guide for inside sales representatives (ISR) in a sales organization.

- Appendix F.1 provides a complete job aid for building a hiring guide.
- Appendix F.2 contains the template for a hiring guide.
- Appendix F.3 contains a complete example of a hiring guide for ISRs in a hypothetical sales organization.

What Is a Hiring Guide?

A hiring guide is a job aid that provides sales recruiters and hiring managers with situational and experience-based questions for assessing a job candidate's critical competencies during the selection process. Using areas of expertise (AOEs) and foundational competencies from the WCSCM to draft questions and define selection criteria ensures accurate and objective assessment of target experiences.

The hiring guide's rating system also provides a consistent framework for comparison of candidates, which is designed to support the selection of the most appropriate candidate for the sales role being filled. An example is also provided for defining a hiring guide for an inside sales representative role.

What Is Needed to Build a Hiring Guide?

You will need the following two documents to create a hiring guide:

- **WCSCM Hiring Guide Template**—Provides the **framework** for building your hiring guide. To create a hiring guide, you will need to customize the WCSCM Hiring Guide Template for the role you select. The following is a brief description of the major sections of the template:
  - **Title**—Identifies the role covered in the hiring guide and the date it was created.
  - **Overview**—Introduces the hiring guide and includes the purpose, organization, guidance on the interview process, a rating key, and an interview scoring summary.
  - **Competency Exploration Worksheet**—Guides the interview discussion and rating in relation to AOEs and foundational competencies.
- **World-Class Sales Competency Model**—This model contains the **AOEs** and **foundational competencies**, as well as their associated key actions, knowledge areas, and skills, which you will use to develop the hiring guide for a specific sales role in the context of your organization.

Appendix F.1—Job Aid for Building a Hiring Guide

Follow the six-step process below to build your hiring guide:

Step 1. Identify the target role and define business requirements for the role.

You may create a hiring guide for sales roles in any of the three parts of the WCSCM; that is, Sales Force, Sales Management and Leadership, and Sales Enablement. In this step, you need to identify the role and, in collaboration with the hiring manager, identify the business requirements for the role.

> **Inside Sales Representative (ISR) Example**—As part of a strategic initiative, a sales organization is redefining the role of the inside sales representative. ISRs are now expected to engage in the end-to-end sales cycle and to proactively identify, qualify, propose, and close opportunities.

After identifying the role and defining business requirements for the role, save the Hiring Guide Template under a new file name. Then, insert the name of the role and other identifying information where indicated by CAPPED text in the WCSCM Hiring Guide Template in Appendix F.2.

Step 2. Identify and select AOEs and foundational competencies.

Referring to the appropriate part (for example, Sales Force) of the WCSCM, identify the most critical AOEs and foundational competencies that meet the hiring requirements identified in the first step of the process. Add the title of the selected AOEs and foundations competencies to the Interview Scoring Summary table in the Hiring Guide template.

TIP: Select only AOEs and foundational competencies that are critical to the role-hiring requirements identified in the first step. Do not include the AOEs and foundational competencies that are not relevant to the sales role in general and/or to the business requirements for candidate selection.

ISR Example—Given the business requirements for hiring ISRs who are capable of identifying, qualifying, proposing, and closing opportunities, the following AOEs and competencies are critical:
- AOEs: **New Account Acquisition** and **Sales Pipeline** and **Forecast Management.**
- Foundational Competencies: Four competencies in the Solution Competencies cluster (that is, Product/Service Acumen, Competitive Intelligence, Consultative Insight, and Negotiating and Gaining Commitment).

Sales Force: Inside Sales Representative	Candidate A	Candidate B	Candidate C
Area of Excellence 1. New Account Acquisition 5. Sales Pipeline and Forecast Management			
Foundational Competency 1. Product/Service Acumen 2. Competitive Intelligence 3. Consultative Insight 4. Negotiating and Gaining Commitment			
Total Number of Points Achieved			

Step 3. Expand the AOE table in the Competency Exploration Worksheet section.

Create a competency description box for each AOE by copying and pasting template rows, as shown.

TIP: The number and titles of AOEs should agree with the list in the Interview Scoring Summary section (Step 2).

Areas of Expertise

AOE 1. New Account Acquisition: *Description*	RATING
Examples: • Key knowledge or skill • Key knowledge or skill	**Question(s):** • **Situation** [Look for . . .] • **[ADVANCED ONLY:] Situation/Question?** [Look for . . .]
NOTES/COMMENTS:	

AOE 5. Sales Pipeline and Forecast Management: *Description*	RATING
Examples: • Key knowledge or skill • Key knowledge or skill	**Question(s):** • **Situation** [Look for . . .] • **[ADVANCED ONLY:] Situation/Question?** [Look for . . .]
NOTES/COMMENTS:	

Step 4. Expand the foundational competencies table in the Competency Exploration Worksheet section.

Repeat Step 4 for the selected foundational competencies. Create a competency description box for each foundational competency by copying and pasting template rows.

TIP: The number and titles of foundational competencies should agree with the list in the Interview Scoring Summary section (Step 2).

Foundational Competencies

Foundational Competency 1. Product/Service Acumen: *Description*	RATING
Examples: • Key action • Key action	**Question(s):** • **Situation** [Look for . . .] • **[ADVANCED ONLY:] Situation/Question?** [Look for . . .]
NOTES/COMMENTS:	

Foundational Competency 2. Competitive Intelligence: *Description*	RATING
Examples: • Key action • Key action	**Question(s):** • **Situation** [Look for . . .] • **[ADVANCED ONLY:] Situation/Question?** [Look for . . .]
NOTES/COMMENTS:	

Foundational Competency 3. Consultative Insight: *Description*	RATING
Examples: • Key action • Key action	**Question(s):** • **Situation** [Look for . . .] • **[ADVANCED ONLY:]** Situation/Question? [Look for . . .]
NOTES/COMMENTS:	

Foundational Competency 4. Negotiating and Gaining Commitment: *Description*	RATING
Examples: • Key action • Key action	**Question(s):** • **Situation** [Look for . . .] • **[ADVANCED ONLY:]** Situation/Question? [Look for . . .]
NOTES/COMMENTS:	

Step 5. Fill in the AOE section of the Competency Exploration Worksheet portion of the template.

Step 5.1. Enter the AOE and its description.

Enter the title of each AOE and its description from the WCSCM.

TIP: You may use the AOE description you find in the WCSCM, or you may customize it to meet your organization's hiring needs and business requirements.

1. New Account Acquisition Pursues opportunities and acquires new accounts by identifying and qualifying opportunities; systematically researching prospects; identifying and prioritizing prospect needs; aligning value propositions with needs and KPIs of prospects; proposing and competitively positioning solutions; and negotiating and closing	RATING
Examples: • Key knowledge or skill • Key knowledge or skill	**Question(s):** • **Situation** [Look for . . .] • **[ADVANCED ONLY:]** Situation/Question? [Look for . . .]
NOTES/COMMENTS:	

Step 5.2. Identify a typical job situation in which an individual in the role would utilize this area of expertise.

Brainstorm a typical experience and then briefly describe it in the "Question(s)" box of the Hiring Guide Template under "Situation." The situation should include an open-ended question or a request that provides an opportunity for the candidate to describe relevant experience(s) and actions that demonstrate his or her expertise.

1. New Account Acquisition Pursues opportunities and acquires new accounts by identifying and qualifying opportunities; systematically researching prospects; identifying and prioritizing prospect needs; aligning value propositions with needs and KPIs of prospects; proposing and competitively positioning solutions; and negotiating and closing	RATING
Examples: • Key knowledge or skill • Key knowledge or skill	**Question(s):** • Tell me about a successful call—a time when you were able to break through a prospect's initial reluctance to buy. • **[ADVANCED ONLY:]** Situation/Question? [Look for . . .]
NOTES/COMMENTS:	

Step 5.3. OPTIONAL: Identify a second job situation in which a more experienced individual in the role would demonstrate this AOE.

Brainstorm an "Advanced" experience and then briefly describe it in the "Question(s)" box of the Hiring Guide Template, under "Situation." The situation should include an open-ended question that provides an opportunity for the candidate to describe relevant experience(s) and actions that demonstrate his or her competency.

1. New Account Acquisition Pursues opportunities and acquires new accounts by identifying and qualifying opportunities; systematically researching prospects; identifying and prioritizing prospect needs; aligning value propositions with needs and KPIs of prospects; proposing and competitively positioning solutions; and negotiating and closing.	RATING
Examples: • Key knowledge or skill • Key knowledge or skill	**Question(s):** • Tell me about a successful call—a time when you were able to break through a prospect's initial reluctance to make a sale. [Look for . . .] • **[ADVANCED ONLY:]** Thorough research of prospective accounts is critical in any sales role. What tools and resources have you used to identify and prioritize potential prospects? [Look for . . .]
NOTES/COMMENTS:	

Step 5.4. Identify criteria for evaluating the interviewee's responses.

Referring to the AOE in the WCSCM, identify key knowledge and key skills for the AOE that the candidate would need to possess to handle the scenario(s) described in the "Question(s)" section. Place them in the "Examples" box next to the questions.

TIP: You may use the knowledge/skills you find in the WCSCM or you may customize additional examples to meet your organization's unique hiring needs.

1. New Account Acquisition	RATING
Pursues opportunities and acquires new accounts by identifying and qualifying opportunities; systematically researching prospects; identifying and prioritizing prospect needs; aligning value propositions with needs and KPIs of prospects; proposing and competitively positioning solutions; and negotiating and closing	

Examples:
- Uses techniques for handling objections and drawbacks
- Adjusts engagement tactics based on a careful reading of a prospect's receptiveness
- Executes hunting efforts with persistence in the face of rejection
- Tracks prospect business and financial health information, including key performance indicators (KPI)
- Generates and manages leads
- Uses opportunity qualification and sizing techniques
- Uses social media sites and connectivity applications
- Identifies the prospect's purchase drivers (e.g., needs, priorities, problems to be solved, or opportunities to be realized)

Question(s):
- Tell me about a successful call—a time when you were able to break through a prospect's initial reluctance to make a sale? [Look for . . .]
- [ADVANCED ONLY:] Thorough research of prospective accounts is critical in any sales role. What tools and resources have you used to identify and prioritize potential customers? [Look for . . .]

NOTES/COMMENTS:

Step 5.5. Add notes for the interviewer after each scenario.

In the "Look for . . ." section after each question, briefly describe the criteria that the interviewer will use to rate the candidate on level of mastery of the AOE.

1. New Account Acquisition	RATING
Pursues opportunities and acquires new accounts by identifying and qualifying opportunities; systematically researching prospects; identifying and prioritizing prospect needs; aligning value propositions with needs and KPIs of prospects; proposing and competitively positioning solutions; and negotiating and closing	

Examples:	Question(s):
• Uses techniques for handling objections and drawbacks • Adjusts engagement tactics based on a careful reading of a prospect's receptiveness • Executes hunting and discovery efforts with persistence in the face of rejection • Tracks prospect business and financial health information, including key performance indicators (KPI) • Generates and manages leads • Uses opportunity qualification and sizing techniques • Uses social media sites and connectivity applications • Identifies prospect's purchase drivers (e.g., needs, priorities, problems to be solved, or opportunities to be realized)	• **Tell me about a successful call—a time when you were able to break through a prospect's initial reluctance to make a sale?** [Look for evidence of the candidates persistence and ability to "think on his/her feet" to handle objections without alienating customer, listen carefully, and adjust tactics based on an accurate reading of the customer's receptiveness.] • **[ADVANCED ONLY:] Thorough research of prospective accounts is critical in any sales role. What tools and resources have you used to identify and prioritize potential customers?** [Look for use of conventional sources, social media, CRM prospect data, industry and company press releases to identify and prioritize likely prospects based on their known business needs, KPIs, challenges, urgency of purchase, authority to buy, and other relevant factors.]

NOTES/COMMENTS:

Step 6. Fill in the foundational competency section of the template.

TIP: The process for creating question scenarios for foundational competencies is nearly the same as that for AOEs; however, in Step 6.4, select criteria from the WCSCM list of Key Actions rather than from Key Knowledge and Key Skills.

Step 6.1. Enter the foundational competency and its description.

Enter the title of each foundational competency and its description from the WCSCM.

TIP: You may use the foundational competency description you find in the WCSCM, or you may customize it to meet your organization's hiring needs.

Step 6.2. Identify a typical job situation in which an individual in the role would demonstrate the foundational competency.

Brainstorm a typical experience and then briefly describe it in the "Question(s)" box of the Hiring Guide template under "Situation." The situation should include an open-ended question or a request that provides an opportunity for the candidate to describe relevant experience(s) and actions that demonstrate his or her competency.

Step 6.3. OPTIONAL: Identify a second job situation in which a more experienced individual in the role would demonstrate the foundational competency.

Brainstorm an "Advanced" experience" and then briefly describe it in the "Question(s)" box of the Hiring Guide Template under "Situation." The situation should include an open-ended question or request that provides an opportunity for the candidate to describe relevant experience(s) and actions that demonstrate his or her competency.

Step 6.4. Identify criteria for evaluating the candidate's responses.

Referring to the WCSCM, identify "Key Actions" for the foundational competency that the candidate would need in order to handle the scenario(s) described in the "Question(s)" section.

TIP: You may use the key actions you find in the WCSCM, or you may customize additional examples to meet your organization's unique hiring needs.

Step 6.5. Add notes for the interviewer after each scenario.

In the "Look for . . ." section after each question, briefly describe the criteria by which the interviewer will judge whether the candidate responses indicate mastery of the foundational competency.

Foundational Competency 1. Product/Service Acumen: Demonstrates a solid understanding of the company's products and solutions and their value proposition	RATING

Examples:	Question(s):
• Maintains a solid understanding of product/solution offerings • Understands solution components and how they add value • Cultivates a range of formal and informal resources for maintaining and developing product/solution knowledge	• **In a rapidly changing technology area, new functionality and business solutions are constantly evolving. How do you maintain your understanding of your organization's portfolio of products and solutions?** [Look for active, self-directed personal development and motivation to stay on top of product and solution offerings and their business benefits. Look, too, for the candidate's initiative in going beyond internal marketing literature to business/technical publications or journals that identify how customers are using current technologies as well as trends and innovations in related products and solutions.] • **[ADVANCED ONLY:] Your customer asked a question this morning about a solution feature that you couldn't answer. You promised an answer tomorrow, but you can't find a quick answer in your usual online sources and the topic turns out to be more complex than you expected. Who or what are your "go-tos" for situations like this?** [This question does not address the candidates' knowledge, but their ability to "know how to find out." Ideally, candidates have nurtured relationships with solution experts, business experts, and mentors who can be called upon for advice or assistance. They should also have built a foundation of knowledge resources through a program of continuous learning.]

NOTES/COMMENTS:

Appendix F.2—Hiring Guide: Template

The purpose of this hiring guide is to help you assess a candidate's critical competencies by exploring his or her experiences in an interview. Accurate and consistent assessment of candidates enables the selection of the most appropriate candidate for the role.

Organization

The hiring guide consists of:

- guidance on how to use selected areas drawn from the World-Class Sales Competency Model (WCSCM)
- the Interview Scoring Summary (to compare multiple candidates for the same role)
- the Competency Exploration Worksheet to guide the discussion, probing, and rating of areas of expertise (AOEs) and foundational competencies.

Guidance on Interview Process

Interviewers will focus on the competencies outlined in the WCSCM. The following steps are suggested for interviewing the candidate:

- Review the definition of the competency. If necessary, refer to the examples provided.
- Explore the candidate's experience in applying the competency. Use the questions provided—or your own—to identify how extensive the candidate's know-how is and to request specific examples.
- Rate the candidate. Use the rating key to determine the extent of the candidate's competency-related experience and write that number in the space provided.
- Determine the total score. Add up the total points achieved by the candidate. Review each question to identify specific strengths or weaknesses, and add summary comments about the candidate.

Note: Due to time limitations or other factors, you may not be able to ask every question provided in the Hiring Guide. It is suggested that you review the complete guide ahead of the interview process and select a subset of questions that are most appropriate for your hiring situation.

Rating Key

Limited	Basic	Moderate	Advanced	Exceptional
1	2	3	4	5

1—Limited: This candidate has very limited experience, if any, with this competency and cannot perform any competency-related tasks.

2—Basic: This candidate has some experience with this competency but needs additional learning and coaching to perform designated competency-related tasks.

3—Moderate: This candidate has practical experience with this competency and can perform some competency-related tasks but requires help and coaching to perform them all.

4—Advanced: This candidate has extensive experience with this competency and can perform all competency-related tasks with no coaching.

5—Exceptional: This candidate is fully experienced in executing on this competency and can coach others to perform the tasks related to this competency.

Interview Scoring Summary

Rating: Rating centers on scoring the extent of the candidate's competency-related knowledge, skills, and actions. Each interviewer should assign every candidate a rating for the competencies examined during the interview (all competencies are listed below).

	Limited 1	Basic 2	Moderate 3	Advanced 4	Exceptional 5

Sales Role	Candidate A	Candidate B	Candidate C
Areas of Expertise • AREA OF EXPERTISE • AREA OF EXPERTISE			
Foundational Competencies • FOUNDATIONAL COMPETENCY • FOUNDATIONAL COMPETENCY			
Total Number of Points Achieved			

Summary Comments
Candidate A: Total Number of Points Achieved: _____ Strengths (Competencies with values of ≥4): _____ Opportunities for Development (Competencies with ≤3): _____ Notes:
Candidate B: Total Number of Points Achieved: _____ Strengths (Competencies with values of ≥4): _____ Opportunities for Development (Competencies with ≤3): _____ Notes:
Candidate C: Total Number of Points Achieved: _____ Strengths (Competencies with values of ≥4): _____ Opportunities for Development (Competencies with ≤3): _____ Notes:

Competency Exploration Worksheet

Areas of Expertise

AEO 1: Description	RATING
Examples: • Key knowledge or skill • Key knowledge or skill	**Question(s):** • **Situation** [Look for . . .] • **[ADVANCED ONLY:]** Situation/Question? [Look for . . .]
NOTES/COMMENTS:	

AEO 1: Description		RATING
Examples: • Key knowledge or skill • Key knowledge or skill	**Question(s):** • **Situation** [Look for . . .] • **[ADVANCED ONLY:]** **Situation/Question?** [Look for . . .]	
NOTES/COMMENTS:		

Foundational Competencies

Foundational Competency: Description		RATING
Examples: • Key action • Key action	**Question(s):** • **Situation** [Look for . . .] • **[ADVANCED ONLY:]** **Situation/Question?** [Look for . . .]	
NOTES/COMMENTS:		

Appendix F.3—Hiring Guide for Inside Sales Representatives: Example

The purpose of this hiring guide is to help you assess a candidate's critical competencies by exploring his or her experiences in an interview. Accurate and consistent assessment of candidates enables the selection of the most appropriate candidate for the role.

Organization

The hiring guide consists of:

- Guidance on how to use selected areas drawn from the World-Class Sales Competency Model (WCSCM)
- The Interview Scoring Summary (to compare multiple candidates for the same role)
- The Competency Exploration Worksheet to guide the discussion, probing, and rating of areas of expertise (AOEs) and foundational competencies.

Guidance on Interview Process

Interviewers will focus on the competencies outlined in the WCSCM. The following steps are suggested for interviewing the candidate:

- **Review the definition of the competency.** If necessary, refer to the examples provided.
- **Explore the candidate's experience in applying the competency.** Use the questions provided—or your own—to identify how extensive the candidate's know-how is and to request specific examples.

- **Rate the candidate.** Use the rating key to determine the extent of the candidate's competency-related experience and write that number in the space provided.
- **Determine total score.** Add up the total points achieved by the candidate. Review each question to identify specific strengths or weaknesses, and add any summary comments about the candidate.

NOTE: Due to time limitations or other factors, you may not be able to ask every question provided in the Hiring Guide. It is suggested that you review the complete guide ahead of the interview process and select a subset of questions that are most appropriate for your hiring situation.

Rating Key

Limited	Basic	Moderate	Advanced	Exceptional
1	2	3	4	5

1—Limited: This candidate has very limited experience, if any, with this competency and cannot perform any competency-related tasks.

2—Basic: This candidate has some experience with this competency but needs additional learning and coaching to perform designated competency-related tasks.

3—Moderate: This candidate has practical experience with this competency and can perform some competency-related tasks, but requires help and coaching to perform them all.

4—Advanced: This candidate has extensive experience with this competency and can perform all competency-related tasks with no coaching.

5—Exceptional: This candidate is fully experienced in executing on this competency and can coach others to perform the tasks related to this competency.

Interview Scoring Summary

Rating: Rating centers on scoring the extent of the candidate's competency-related knowledge, skills, and actions. Each interviewer should assign every candidate a rating for the competencies examined during the interview (all competencies are listed below).

Limited	Basic	Moderate	Advanced	Exceptional
1	2	3	4	5

Sales Role	Candidate A	Candidate B	Candidate C
Areas of Expertise 1. New Account Acquisition 5. Sales Pipeline and Forecast Management			
Foundational Competencies 1. Product / Service Acumen 2. Competitive Intelligence 3. Consultative Insight 4. Negotiating and Gaining Commitment			
Total Number of Points Achieved			

Summary Comments
Candidate A: Total Number of Points Achieved: _____ Strengths (Competencies with values of ≥4): _____ Opportunities for Development (Competencies with ≤3): _____ Notes:
Candidate B: Total Number of Points Achieved: _____ Strengths (Competencies with values of ≥4): _____ Opportunities for Development (Competencies with ≤3): _____ Notes:
Candidate C: Total Number of Points Achieved: _____ Strengths (Competencies with values of ≥4): _____ Opportunities for Development (Competencies with ≤3): _____ Notes:

Competency Exploration Worksheet Rating

Areas of Expertise

1. New Account Acquisition—Pursues opportunities and acquires new accounts by identifying and qualifying opportunities; systematically researching prospects; identifying and prioritizing prospect needs; aligning value propositions with needs and KPIs of prospects; proposing and competitively positioning solutions; and negotiating and closing	**RATING**

Examples:	**Question(s):**
• Uses techniques for handling objections and drawbacks • Adjusts engagement tactics based on a careful reading of a prospect's receptiveness • Executes hunting and discovery efforts with persistence in the face of rejection • Tracks prospect business and financial health information, including key performance indicators (KPI) • Generates and manages leads • Uses opportunity qualification and sizing techniques • Uses social media sites and connectivity applications • Identifies the prospect's purchase drivers (e.g., needs, priorities, problems to be solved, or opportunities to be realized)	• **Tell me about a successful call—a time when you were able to break through a prospect's initial reluctance to make a sale?** [Look for evidence of the candidates persistence and ability to "think on his/her feet" to handle objections without alienating customer, listen carefully, and adjust tactics based on an accurate reading of the customer's receptiveness.] • **[ADVANCED ONLY:] Thorough research of prospective accounts is critical in any sales role. What tools and resources have you used to identify and prioritize potential customers?** [Look for use of conventional sources, social media, CRM prospect data, industry and company press releases to identify and prioritize likely prospects based on their known business needs, KPIs, challenges, urgency of purchase, authority to buy, and other relevant factors.]

NOTES/COMMENTS:

Competency Exploration Worksheet Rating (continued)

5. Sales Pipeline and Forecast Management—Leverages the power of sales analytics to exploit sales opportunities and ensure achievement of business results by populating and managing the sales pipeline; managing and protecting margin; developing and monitoring sales forecasts; and utilizing customer relationship management (CRM) systems	RATING

Examples:

- Tracks company's pricing guidelines, including discount and approval process
- Focuses on margin requirements when qualifying opportunities and prospects to ensure profitability
- Uses integrated CRM systems to enter relevant information for forecasting, resource allocation, and decision making

Question(s):

- **Tell me about your experience with CRM (customer relationship management) tools. How does CRM fit into your daily practice and in what ways has CRM contributed to your success?** [Candidates should have experience using CRM to automate, integrate, and expedite a variety of sales tasks. Contributions to success will vary but may relate to tracking/measuring promotion campaigns, assessing customer spend and churn, prioritizing around customer KPIs, synchronizing schedules and appointments, communicating with customers, improving customer experiences, coordinating planning and pursuit activities with partners. Look for specific links to business impacts (e.g., customer satisfaction, successful pursuits with partners.)]

- **[ADVANCED ONLY:] Ensuring bottom-line profitability through margin management and competitive pricing is an important part of any sales role. Provide a couple of examples of when you have successfully executed margin management strategies at either the account or opportunity level.** [Look for a focus on margin-rich opportunities and appropriate application of pricing tools and parameters in negotiations. The candidate may also mention specific techniques, including up-selling, cross-selling, discounts, product mix, use of third-party or legacy products, and add-ons.]

NOTES/COMMENTS:

Foundational Competencies

Foundational Competency 1. Product/Service Acumen: Demonstrates a solid understanding of the company's products and solutions and their value proposition	RATING

Examples:	Question(s):
• Maintains a solid understanding of product/ solution offerings • Understands solution components and how they add value • Cultivates a range of formal and informal resources for maintaining and developing product/solution knowledge	• **In a rapidly changing technology area, new functionality and business solutions are constantly evolving. How do you maintain your understanding of your organization's portfolio of products and solutions?** [Look for active, self-directed personal development and motivation to stay on top of product and solution offerings and their business benefits. Look, too, for the candidate's initiative in going beyond internal marketing literature to business/technical publications or journals that identify how customers are using current technologies as well as trends and innovations in related products and solutions.] • **[ADVANCED ONLY:] Your customer asked a question this morning about a solution feature that you couldn't answer. You promised an answer tomorrow, but you can't find a quick answer in your usual online sources and the topic turns out to be more complex than you expected. Who or what are your "go-tos" for situations like this?** [This question does not address the candidates' knowledge, but their ability to "know how to find out." Ideally, candidates have nurtured relationships with solution experts, business experts, and mentors who can be called upon for advice or assistance. They should also have built a foundation of knowledge resources through a program of continuous learning.]

NOTES/COMMENTS:

Competency Exploration Worksheet Rating (continued)

Foundational Competency 2. Competitive Intelligence: Applies competitive insight to effectively differentiate and position solutions	RATING

Examples:	Question(s):
• Stays current with the competitive landscape • Ensures that competitor claims are appropriately vetted in solution definition and planning • Understands competitors' strategies and tactics	• Having an in-depth knowledge of the competitive landscape is critical to differentiating and positioning solutions. Tell me what actions you take to maintain current knowledge of competitors' strategies and tactics, as well as the strengths and weaknesses of their product? [Interviewees should describe sources, strategies, networks, and activities they use to build competitor knowledge on an on-going basis. Look for proactive research as well as monitoring of overall industry trends.] • [ADVANCED ONLY:] Describe a highly competitive sales pursuit in which careful differentiation and positioning of your solution led to a positive outcome. What aspects of your strategy and messaging were most effective and why? [Candidates should demonstrate careful vetting and addressing of competitor claims. Strategy and counter-tactics used in the example should be based on a comprehensive understanding of strategy and tactics.]

NOTES/COMMENTS:

Foundational Competency 3. Consultative Insight: Provides the informed experience, breadth of insight, and robust exploration essential for helping customers to make an optimum decision	RATING

Examples:	Question(s):
• Challenges the customer by providing a wider perspective to solution definition • Ensures that solutions are justified and in the best interest of the customer • Ensures that the proposed solutions satisfy customer needs	• In this role, you will be expected to build consultative relationships with your clients. Tell me about a time when you challenged a customer with a solution alternative that broadened your customer's thinking about new developments and opportunities. How did you work with the customer to determine if the solution was a good fit? [Candidates should demonstrate knowledge of trends and developments in the customer's business but should also evaluate the range of solution alternatives in terms of their impact on solving the customer's business challenges. Also, look for evidence that the interviewee worked with the customer to identify any risks associated with the solution.] • [ADVANCED ONLY:] Think of a time when a customer deliberated between a forward-leaning solution with new potential benefits and a "safer," more traditional solution. How did you guide your customer to the best decision? [Here, the candidate's response should emphasize that the best solution is the one that best meets the customer's needs. The consultant's role should be described as not only to introduce solution alternatives but also to determine their impact on solving business challenges and to identify risks to achievement of the customer's goals.]

NOTES/COMMENTS:

Foundational Competency 4. Negotiating and Gaining Commitment: Helps align all stakeholder interests to create a win/win balance that demonstrates mutual benefit, increases the probability of commitment, and drives the opportunity to closure	RATING

Examples:

- Effectively plans and prepares for negotiations
- Determines optimum bargaining position
- Builds value propositions
- Applies appropriate techniques to reach agreements

Question(s):

- You have a meeting scheduled with a colleague that you're partnering with and key customer stakeholders. Your goal is to negotiate the last details of the deal and gain the customer's commitment. Are you ready? Tell me what's on your checklist. [The "checklist" should indicate that the candidate has defined a negotiating strategy; prepared the team (that is, partnering colleague); aligned the solution to key decision makers' criteria; identified critical points and justifications to make; determined valid expectation and desired outcomes; and defined a walk-away position.]
- [ADVANCED ONLY:] Describe a situation in which you walked away from a negotiation without gaining the customer's commitment. What was your thought process in making your decision? [Of critical importance here is advanced determination of valid expectations and desired outcomes as well as a walk-away position. Other actions that demonstrate effective negotiation technique include defining a negotiating strategy, preparing the team, aligning the solution with key decision makers' criteria for success, correctly interpreting of signals, emphasizing critical points, and providing justification.]

NOTES/COMMENTS:

APPENDIX G

TOOLS AND TEMPLATES FOR INDIVIDUALS TO USE THE ATD WCSCM

The new ATD World-Class Sales Competency Model (WCSCM) not only provides sales organizations with a state-of-the-art competency framework that can be used as a critical tool to achieve a variety of sales talent management goals, but it also provides individuals with a framework for their own competency development.

This appendix provides the following tools for individuals to effectively use the WCSCM:

- Appendix G.1—Template for building a customized AOE self-assessment
- Appendix G.2—Template for building a customized foundational competency self-assessment
- Appendix G.3—Template for the ATD WCSCM Individual Development Plan (IDP).

Appendix G.1—Building a Customized AOE Self-Assessment: Template

Instructions

This template consists of two parts: current role AOEs and desired role AOEs.

Part 1: Current Role

- Select AOEs aligned with your current role and add key knowledge areas and skills.
- Record the importance ratings from Appendix D, provided by participants in the survey.
- Rate yourself.
- Subtract your self-ratings from the importance ratings provided by survey participants.

AOE: Title	Importance Rating	Self-Rating	Gap
Key Knowledge Areas: Average for all	Average	Average	
Item			
Item			
Item			
Item			
Item			
Item			
Item			
Item			
Key Skills: Average for all	Average	Average	
Item			
Item			
Item			
Item			
Item			
Item			
Item			
Item			

Part 2: Desired Role

- Select AOEs aligned with your desired role and add key knowledge areas and skills from those AOEs.
- Record the importance ratings from Appendix D, provided by participants in the survey.
- Rate yourself.
- Subtract your self-ratings from the importance ratings provided by survey participants.

AOE: Title	Importance Rating	Self-Rating	Gap
Key Knowledge Areas: Average for all	Average	Average	
Item			
Item			
Item			
Item			
Item			
Item			
Item			
Item			
Key Skills: Average for all	Average	Average	
Item			
Item			
Item			
Item			
Item			
Item			
Item			
Item			

Appendix G.2—Building a Customized Foundational Competency Self-Assessment: Template

Instructions

- Rate yourself using the following the 5-point scale:
  - 1—Strong Development Need
  - 2—Development Need
  - 3—Opportunity for Growth
  - 4—Solid Strength
  - 5—Strength to Leverage.
- Subtract your self-ratings from the importance ratings provided by survey participants.

Foundational Competency Cluster: Collaboration	Importance	Self-Rating	Gap
Relationship Building Competency	Average for competency **4.5**	Average for competency	Average for competency
Actively nurtures positive relationships	4.5		
Develops and leverages relationships to achieve results	4.4		
Protects the integrity of relationships	4.5		
Foundational Competency: Title	Average for competency	Average for competency	Average for competency
Key Action			
Key Action			
Key Action			
Foundational Competency: Title	Average for competency	Average for competency	Average for competency
Key Action			
Key Action			
Key Action			
Foundational Competency: Title	Average for competency	Average for competency	Average for competency
Key Action			
Key Action			
Key Action			

Appendix G.3—Individual Development Plan (IDP) Template

Use the following template to create an individual development plan, based on the ATD WCSCM.

Name:		Date:	
Current Role	Desired Role		
Current Role AOEs and Knowledge and Skill to Be Developed			
AOE Title	**AOE Knowledge and Skill to Be Developed**	**Learning and Development Options**	**Timeframe**
1.			
2.			
3.			
Desired Role AOEs and Knowledge and Skill to Be Developed			
AOE Title	**AOE Knowledge and Skill to Be Developed**	**Learning and Development Options**	**Timeframe**
1.			
2.			
Foundational Competencies to Be Developed			
Foundational Competency Title		**Learning and Development Options**	**Timeframe**
1.			
2.			
3.			
4.			
5.			
6.			

REFERENCES

Adamson, B., and M. Dixon. 2011. *The Challenger Sale: Taking Control of the Customer Conversation.* New York: Penguin.

Adamson, B., and N. Toman. 2012. "The End of Solution Sales." *Harvard Business Review,* July-August. hbr.org/2012/07/the-end-of-solution-sales.

Association for Talent Development (ATD). 2015. *The Mobile Landscape 2015: Building Toward Anytime, Anywhere Learning.* Alexandria, VA: ATD Press.

Bernthal, P., K. Colteryahn, P. Davis, J. Naughton, W. Rothwell, and R. Wellins. 2004. *ASTD 2004 Competency Study: Mapping the Future: New Workplace Learning and Performance Competencies.* Alexandria, VA: ASTD Press.

Davie, C., T. Stephenson, and M.V. de Uster. 2010. "Three Trends in Business-to-Business Sales." *Insights & Publications,* May. McKinsey & Company. www.mckinsey.com /insights/marketing_sales/three_trends_in_business-to-business_sales.

Elmgren, B. 2013. "The Future of Organizational Learning." Saskatchewan Association of Human Resource Professionals, September 18. www.slideshare.net/BrettElmgren /the-future-of-organizational-learning.

Fry, R. 2015. "Millennials Surpass Gen Xers as the Largest Generation in U.S. Labor Force." Pew Research Center. Fact Tank, May 11. www.pewresearch.org/fact -tank/2015/05/11/millennials-surpass-gen-xers-as-the-largest-generation-in-u-s-labor -force/.

Goldman, G., and E. Kelly. 2014. "Business Trends 2014: Navigating the Next Wave of Globalization." Deloitte University Press. www.mahbubani.net/interviews /Global%20BusinessTrends2014.pdf.

Kelly, E. 2014. "Business Trends 2014: Navigating the Next Wave of Globalization." Deloitte University Press. www.mahbubani.net/interviews/Global%20Busi-nessTrends2014.pdf.

Lambert, B., T. Ohai, and E. Kerkhoff. 2009. *World-Class Selling: New Sales Competencies.* Alexandria, VA: ASTD Press.

Ledingham, D., M. Kovac, L. Beaudin, and S.D. Burton. 2014. "Mastering the New Reality of Sales." *Bain Brief,* April 9. www.bain.com/publications/articles/mastering-the-new-reality-of-sales.aspx.

Lockwood, N.R. 2006. "Talent Management: Driver for Organizational Success." *SHRM Research Quarterly.* Alexandria, VA: Society for Human Resource Management. www.shrm.org/research/articles/articles/documents/0606rquartpdf.pdf.

Martin, S. 2012. "Top 10 Sales Trends for 2013." *Harvard Business Review,* December 10. hbr.org/2012/12/top-10-sales-trends-for-2013.

McLagan, P., and R. McCullough. 1983. *Models for Excellence: The Conclusions and Recommendations of the ASTD Training and Development Competency Study.* Alexandria, VA.

McLagan, P., and D. Suhadolnik, 1991. *Models for HRD Practice: The Research Report.* Alexandria, VA: American Society for Training and Development.

Mitchell, A. 2013. "The Rise of the Millennial Workforce." *Wired.* www.wired.com/2013/08/the-rise-of-the-millennial-workforce.

Moore, K. 2011. "How Sales Is Totally Different From 10 Years Ago: RIP the Sales Funnel." *Forbes,* August 1. www.forbes.com/sites/karlmoore/2015/06/15/five-click-leadership-how-introverts-can-get-ahead/.

Moritz, B., R. Gittings, and T. Craren. 2014. "Good to Grow: 2014 US CEO Survey." PricewaterhouseCoopers Research Report. www.pwc.com/us/en/ceo-survey-us/2014/assets/2014-us-ceo-survey.pdf.

Peacock, M. 2012, "Mobile Is the New Face of Customer Engagement, Forrester Says." CMS Wire White Paper, February 15. www.cmswire.com/cms/customer-experience/mobile-is-the-new-face-of-customer-engagement-forrester-says-014522.php.

Pinto, P., and J. Walker. 1978. *A Study of Professional Training and Development Roles and Competencies.* Madison, WI: ASTD.

Piskurich, G., and E. Sanders. 1998. *ASTD Models for Learning Technologies: Roles, Competencies, and Outputs.* Alexandria, VA: ASTD Press.

Porter, K. 2013. "Twelve Skills You Need to Keep Your Job in Sales." Salesforce.com Blog, April 22. www.salesforce.com/blog/2013/04/12-skills-you-need-to-keep-your-job-in-sales.html.

Rothwell, W. 1996. *ASTD Models for Human Performance Improvement: Roles, Competencies, and Outputs.* Alexandria, VA: ASTD Press.

———, E. Sanders, and J. Soper. 1999. *ASTD Models for Workplace Learning and Performance: Roles, Competencies, and Outputs.* Alexandria, VA: ASTD Press.

Rothwell, W.J., J. Arneson, and J. Naughton. 2013. *ASTD Competency Study: The Training & Development Profession Redefined*. Alexandria, VA: ASTD Press.

Russo, C. 2014. "Three of the Biggest Sales Training Trends." Salesforce Search, April 4. www.salesforcesearch.com/bid/160428/3-of-the-Biggest-Sales-Training-Trends.

Schadler, T., J.C. McCarthy, M. Brown, H. Martyn, and R. Brown. 2012. "Mobile Is the New Face of Customer Engagement." Forrester Research, February 13. www.forrester.com/Mobile+Is+The+New+Face+Of+Engagement/fulltext/-/E-RES60544?docid=60544.

Schawbel, D. 2012. "Millennials vs. Baby Boomers: Who Would You Rather Hire?" *Time*, March 29. business.time.com/2012/03/29/millennials-vs-baby-boomers-who-would-you-rather-hire.

Verazi, K. 2010. "The Future of Organizational Learning." Big Task Weekend. www.bigtaskweekend.com/the-future-of-organizational-learning.html.

Wesson, M. 2014. "The Smart Guide to Social Selling." Salesforce.com Blog, May 9. www.salesforce.com/blog/2014/05/free-e-book-the-smart-guide-to-social-selling-.html.

PROJECT TEAM

Project Contributors		
ATD and Productivity Dynamics, Inc. would like to thank the following individuals for their respective contributions to the World-Class Sales Competency Model (WCSCM).		
Joe Anzalone	Brian Groth	Paul Petroski
Michele Aymold	Tom Hunter	Angelo Picucci
Katherine Bain	Mike Kunkle	Ian Platt
Michael Barke	Ryan Leavitt	Naomi Price
Jim Barone	Melissa Madian	Kelly Riggs
Karen Clay Basile	Carlos Madriz	Nick Saban
Guido Bohler	Greg Madsen	Blake Scanlon
Kara Brinkerhoff	Ragi Mahmoud	Vishal Shah
Alfredo Castro	Tom Manos	Greg Stack
Claude Chadillon	Mark McCarthy	Keith Stoneman
Glenn Clark	Misha McPherson	Elinor Stutz
Leonard Cochran	Marci Meaux	Babette Ten Haken
Jenny Dearborn	Mark Meredith	Zan Terry
Carole Dommee	Mike Milbourn	Robert (Bob) Terson
Leanne Drennan	Amanda Miller	Tracy Tibedo
Kevin Elmore	Andy Miller	Michael Trow
Toni Ferbrache	Adrian Morales	Chris Tung
Drew Fleming	Barry Murphy	Denver White
Joe Galvin	Tim Ohai	George Yang
Shane Gibson	Don Perrotta	

PROJECT TEAM

Initiative Teams	
Association for Talent Development (ATD)	**Productivity Dynamics, Inc.**
Roxy Torres | Manager, Sales Enablement Community Jennifer Naughton | Sr. Director, Credentialing David Frankel | Research Specialist	Reza Sisakhti | Research Director Alison Fox | Senior Research Analyst Rande Neukam | Senior Research Analyst Joyce Nadeau | Project Manager

ABOUT THE AUTHOR

 **Reza Sisakhti,** PhD, is the managing director of Productivity Dynamics, a research and consulting firm dedicated to helping clients achieve significant business results through the creation of effective learning and performance environments. For more than two decades, Reza has been creating business-essential competency models and measuring the business impact of training programs for major corporations such as Chevron, Cisco, Ernst & Young, HP, IBM, Intuit, and Verizon.